Activities That Teach Family Values

Activities That Teach Family Values

by Tom Jackson, M.Ed.

Red Rock Publishing

Credits
Cover Design: Bill Kuhre, Kuhre Ad Art
Cover Photo: John Jackson
Editing: Frank Jackson
Illustrations: Greg Bitney
Page Design and Typesetting: Accu-Type Typographers
Printing: Publisher's Press

First Printing 1998
Second Printing 1999
Third Printing 2002

ISBN 0-9664633-0-7

Additional copies of this book and other materials by Tom Jackson may be ordered from your supplier or from:
Active Learning Center, Inc.
3835 West 800 North
Cedar City UT 84720
(435) 586-7058 between the hours of 7:00 a.m. and 7:00 p.m. Mountain Time
FAX: (435) 586-0185
Toll free: 1-888-588-7078 between the hours of 7:00 a.m. and 7:00 p.m. Mountain Time

Web site: www.activelearning.org

Have Tom Jackson speak to your organization or conference. Call for information.

Contents

Activities

From the Author
Tom Jackson

Hello, my name is Tom Jackson and my wife's name is Janet. Yes, that makes her Janet Jackson. No, not the one that sings! We have been married for twenty-six years (as of 1999) and have raised three children. Our oldest is Frank, who married Traci from Salt Lake City. Our middle child is Brent who married Julie from right here in Cedar City. Our youngest is Denise, who married Cody from Boulder, a small cattle town in Utah. Brent and Julie gave us our first grandchild, Andy, in July of 1997. Their little Emily is our fifth grandchild. Frank and Traci have twin sons, Alex and Jason. And Denise and Cody have red-headed Bailey Kay. All of our kids have moved into their own homes, but they come to visit often and we enjoy watching them as they are raising their families. We have lived in both urban and rural areas and have enjoyed both settings. Our family loves the great outdoors and southern Utah provides us with plenty of opportunities to enjoy nature at its best.

I wanted you to know a little bit about my family since our children have influenced Janet and me in the way we feel about parenting and the teaching of values. We used many activities, similar to the ones found in this book, with our children to help teach them values.

My professional background includes a Master's Degree in Education from the University of Southern California. I spent 12 years as a high school teacher in southern California as well as the coach of the boys' and girls' cross country and track teams. I then spent 13 years as a prevention specialist for a mental health/alcohol and drug center in southwestern Utah. During this time, I also served on the

Utah State Office of Education Steering Committee for Alcohol and
Other Drug Education and on the Governor of Utah's Substance Abuse
and Anti-Violence Coordinating Council. Janet and I together served
for ten years as the Youth Directors at our church for the seventh
through twelfth grades youth program. In all of these positions I was
able to work with hundreds of children and youth to help teach them
the skills they need to survive in today's world.

Today I am the director of the Active Learning Center, Inc. which
distributes my books. My first two books, *Activities That Teach*
and *More Activities That Teach*, as well as a number of magazine
articles and other publications, were written to help the classroom
teacher and other people who work with children and youth teach life
skills in a creative and effective manner. I also direct the Active
Learning Foundation, a nonprofit corporation which handles my
speaking engagements around the country where I conduct workshops on how to use activities to teach life skills and values.

Janet and I wish you all the best as you take on the challenge of raising your children. Have fun with these activities and may God bless
you and your family!

Acknowledgments

No one creates a book in a vacuum or develops their philosophy of life without being influenced through their interaction with others. Some of those who have helped me shape my thoughts about how to help families and how to use activities to teach are Mary Lou Bozich, Bev Campbell, Mike Cottam, Carrie Cox, Merlin Goode, Judy Humiston, Verne Larsen, Nikki Lovell, Neal Smith, Shelly Stevens and Sherry Young. I thank all of you who have encouraged me to share my activities with others and those who have suggested activities to me. I also owe a lot to both Janet's parents, Phyllis and Donald, and my parents, Minola and Bill, for sharing their values with both Janet and me. My own family has been wonderful in supporting my efforts in writing this book. While growing up, our children, Frank, Brent and Denise, have been my teachers and test subjects for many of the approaches I have found successful in the area of teaching values. My wife, Janet, is the hub which our family revolves around, the rock on which I depend and my best friend. There is no way to adequately thank her for all she has done for our family and for me. I thank God for giving me the wonderful family that I have and blessing me as I follow my dreams.

Introduction

The word "values" means different things to different people. The activities in this book won't try to tell you what to think, but they will give you a chance to share what you believe with your children and have fun at the same time.

Most people have three options when choosing how to share their values with their children. The first option is by example: you live your life in such a way that your children will be able to tell what you believe by how you act. A second method is by lecturing: you can simply tell them what you think and be done with it. A third method is to use teachable moments. With this approach, you wait for a situation to occur and then use those circumstances to share your beliefs with your children. All three of these options have problems. What if your actions don't always exactly reflect your beliefs? What if your children tune out your lectures? What if the right teachable moment never arrives?

This book gives you another choice. You can bring the family together and have fun engaging in an activity that will allow you to create your own teachable moments. Then you can spend time talking with each other about what took place in the activity and how that can relate to "real life." It's easy to do. The activities are written in a user-friendly format with easy-to-follow instructions. There are even suggested discussion questions you can use to help bring your message home. It couldn't be any easier!

It doesn't matter if you are a single parent with one child or have a house full of children, if your kids are in the critical years then your family will benefit from these activities. You won't find a lot of parenting advice in this book. There are plenty of parenting books you can buy if that is your need. However, if you want to open up the lines of communication with your children, strengthen your relationships, teach them values and have fun at the same time, then you chose the right book. So turn the pages and get started.

CHAPTER ONE

Me Teach Values?
You've Got To Be Kidding!

Your kid comes through the door after spending the day at school, heads for the kitchen and opens the refrigerator. You enthusiastically ask, "How was school today?" The answer is a non-committal "Fine" or simply a series of grunts, groans and shrugs. Of course, you could follow this up with that age old question, "What did you learn in school today?" but if you do be prepared to hear the equally age old answer of "Nothing." I use these examples to simply illustrate the difficulties of communicating with our children and teens.

To further illustrate what I mean by communication problems, let me relate a personal story about Brent, our middle child. He came home from high school one day and I asked him, "Did anything exciting happen at school today?" He answered with the typical series of grunts and shrugs. The next day I went to his high school on a business matter and found out that there had been a fire in his chemistry class the day before. So that night I said, "Brent, yesterday when I asked you about your day you told me nothing exciting had happened. Well today I found out that there was a fire in your chemistry class." He replied, "Yeah, but we didn't get to go home!" So you see, I didn't ask the right question. Brent thought it would be exciting to go home, but a classroom fire is nothing out of the ordinary.

Every newspaper article, magazine story, book or talk on parenting always emphasizes the importance of good communication between parent and child. Communication has been offered as the solution to self-esteem problems, feeling unloved, drug use, gangs, etc. That is all well and good, but how does this take place? When we buy a car we get an owner's manual. When we buy a clock radio we get a set of operating instructions. When we have a baby we get congratulated. Soon you begin to ask, "Where is the manual?" and "What am I supposed to do with this kid?" Every survey that asks parents "What do you want for your child?" will show the top answer as "I just want them to be happy in life!" That's great, but the next question has to be "What do I do to help them become happy?" Linda and Richard Eyre, in their book *Teaching Your Children Values,* answer this question when they state, "We should teach values to our children because it is the most significant and effective thing we can do for their happiness."

We all want our kids to have good values, but values don't come easily. Some will say that they don't have to teach values because their kids will just learn them as they grow up. These people are right. However, whose values are they learning? Many studies have documented the hundreds of hours of television our kids are exposed to each year. A study by BJK&E Media Group reported that 40% of children ages 6 – 11 have televisions in their bedrooms. Does television share the same values that you have? Values are very personal. This book does not attempt to teach values from any certain point of view. It is a collection of activities that you can use to teach your own set of values. The activities provide the format, the structure and the fun, you provide the substance.

Teaching values is not something you do to kids, it's something you do with kids. A good friend of mine, Verne Larsen, addressed this issue with the following statement, "Kids don't need more things to do, they need more adults to do things with." Our society talks a lot about "quality time" vs. "quantity time". To be honest, neither one of these will serve you when trying to teach values. What you will need is effective time. We seem to be obsessed with speed today, whether it be fast food or faster computers. Values, however, must be shared with our children, not force fed to them. It can not be done quickly or through some magic formula. The activities in this book will give you an opportunity to spend whatever available time you have with your children and teens more effectively. It really doesn't matter if the outcome of the activity is a success or not, what really matters is the time we spend sharing thoughts and experiences. To really teach values we have to stop lecturing and start sharing our opinions and feelings about this most important area of development.

In the book *20 Teachable Virtues,* Barbara Unell and Jerry Wyckoff state, "Currently, talk about virtue, values, morals and character has emerged in the forefront of the movement for social change. However, it is important to understand that these traits must be taught rather than talked." By using activities as a catalyst for teaching values, you have a built-in method to encourage communication within your family. Participating in an activity and then talking about it is a lot easier than sitting your kids down on the couch and saying, "Well kids, today I would like to address the issue of honesty, so listen carefully." Family relations expert Dr. Judith Bunge of Ohio State University said, "We believe children learn best by being actively involved." My wife and I know from personal experience that lecturing doesn't change behavior, but experiencing an activity together and then sharing our thoughts about it can, over time, make a real impact.

You will notice that I labeled the years from 7½ to 15½ as the critical years. These ages are just an estimate. Your children may have matured differently than my estimate. The reason I chose these ages was that before the age of 7½ most kids can't easily discuss the concepts that are introduced in these activities. Why choose 15½ as the other end? Have you ever tried to discuss something with a teenager who is about to get their driver's license? They are entering the expert years. For the next few years they will know it all and will be glad to tell you whatever you need to know. So I encourage you to get the values message in early. It doesn't mean your kids will grow up to accept your values, but at least it will give them a standard by which to measure their own values. Another friend of mine, Don Shaw, said "There is a 96% chance that your kids will grow up to be just like you." Scary thought, isn't it?

This book isn't an owner's manual on how-to raise kids, but hopefully it will be a fun way to help you teach your children and teens the values they need to be happy and to succeed in today's difficult and increasingly complex world. So have fun and enjoy the journey!

"Parents can only give good advice or put them on the right paths, but the final forming of a person's character lies in their own hands." Anne Frank

CHAPTER TWO

Teaching Values

Values influence the way we view the world, the decisions we make and ultimately our behavior itself. I feel that values drive our decisions which in turn drive our behavior. Let me give you an example. Let's say that a high school student values education and wants to go to college. He has a big test on Friday morning. Some of his friends call him up on Thursday night and invite him to a pizza party and watch a video. If he truly values education, then his decision will be not to go for pizza and he will stay home and study. If he actually values fun over education, then his decision will be to go to the party. Positive values produce positive choices, while negative values could result in negative choices. People such as teachers, friends, religious figures, neighbors and other influences such as music, television, videos, etc. all contribute to teaching values. However, parents can be the most critical factor in the teaching of values.

Here are seven questions you can ask yourself to see if you are succeeding in teaching values to your children and teens.

1. Do you know what your own values are?

2. Are you consistent in what you say and do, or do you say one thing and behave differently?

3. Do your children clearly understand what your beliefs and values are?

4. What opportunities do you provide to share your values with your children?

5. Do you provide opportunities for your children to discuss values and reflect on how they impact everyday life?

6. Are the rules of your house consistent with the values that you have?

7. Do you reinforce positive behavior that reflects values that you believe in?

By answering this list of questions, you have already made a good start in providing values training to your children. Values are a way of life, so you must incorporate the teaching of them into all aspects of your life. This can't be a "do as I say" kind of thing. Your role modeling plays a very important part in the passing of values from one generation to the next. Without you modeling the appropriate kinds of behavior, all the lectures, discussions and activities in the world will not make enough of a difference that your children will be encouraged to adopt the values that you talk about but don't believe enough in to live by.

"Whatever you would have your children become, strive to exhibit in your own lives and conversation."
Lydia H. Sigourney

CHAPTER THREE

Using Activities to Teach Values

The activities in this book will give you the tools to help you raise what all parents want: happy kids who consider their lives a success and make positive contributions to our society. The activities provide you with a forum to discuss what is on your mind in a non-threatening fashion. I don't expect the completion of any one activity to change the course of your child's future, but each activity will provide another building block. Put enough building blocks together and you have a solid foundation on which your child can steer his or her life course. I will promise you this: the more activities you do, the more impact they will make. The activities are not placed in the order that you should use them. They are simply alphabetized. Rather, complete the activities that deal with topics about which you have the most concern. How often you undertake an activity is also up to you. Even though I have chosen fifty-two activities, that doesn't mean that you have to do one per week.

As parents you can't tell your kids how to think, but you can give them something to think about and a direction that you would like for them to head. This is the age old argument of "control vs. influence." I feel that while parents can't control their child's thinking, they do have a lot of influence. By working through an activity, discussing how it applies to a value that you hold and then allowing your child to observe you as you live that value in your daily life, you can have a great deal of influence.

Don't worry if you feel inadequate as a teacher. The activities are completely developed and ready to use. All you need to do is add kids! The basic format for conducting an activity would consist of some introductory comments from you, followed by the activity itself and ending with a discussion. Be sure that you read completely through each activity before you try it with your family. Go over each step in your mind and understand it before you begin. To help understand the concept of the activity, read through the questions at the end to see how the activity could be discussed.

Introduce the activities with a fun-filled attitude. If you approach the activity full of enthusiasm, so will your family. Don't let these activities become bogged down by a heavy handed approach to values. Remember that your kids probably don't equate learning with fun. So the first couple of times you call them together for an activity, they may be less than thrilled. Start with some of the more exciting activities to get them hooked. Soon they will learn that you can talk about values and have fun at the same time!

It is not about flawlessly completing the activity! This book contains fifty-two activities. Each one is designed to help you teach about values. Too many people get caught up in having the activity be perfect, when what we are really trying to do is simply use the activity to make it easier to talk about the value. If the activity doesn't work out exactly as planned, it really doesn't matter. You can still discuss what happened and open up the value discussion. Instead of worrying, enjoy the time you are spending with your family. It is these shared experiences that enhance the relationships within a family and draw you all closer together. When these relationships are strong, there is a much greater likelihood that your children will accept your values and words of wisdom that you share with them.

CHAPTER FOUR

The Values Themselves

I have chosen seven universal values to organize this book and the activities around. The seven values are Responsibility, Respect, Honesty, Perseverance, Cooperation, Caring and Service to Others. These seven values seem to be universally accepted as important for our children and youth to possess. However, this is an artificially short list in the sense that there are many other values that we also desire our children and youth to exhibit.

As you look at the activity outline you will see that I have listed one of these universal values at the top of each activity. This simply means that the activity can be categorized under that value. However, when you read the concept and key words, you will recognize there are many other values that the activity also addresses. For example, you will see manners under respect, you will find goal setting under perseverance, you will find family bonding under caring, etc. Many times values do not fit easily or comfortably under just one heading. By choosing just seven values in which to organize this book, I had to include a number of other values under each of the seven categories.

This approach gives you a chance to make each activity meet the needs of your family. You can concentrate on the value that is listed under the topic heading or you can address one or more of the words listed as key words. The magic of an activity is that it can be applied in so many different ways. Feel free to use any application that works best for you and your family. As I looked at other books on teaching values to children, I was struck by the fact that many of them give you a specific approach and detailed definition to each value they listed. My approach is somewhat different. I want each value to be defined by you and explained in a manner that is consistent with how you would like it to be expressed by your family members. This will make the activities not only unique for each family that uses them, but universal in their application regardless of your beliefs, race, creed, culture, or nationality.

CHAPTER FIVE

Understanding the Activity Lesson Plan

Value: This will give you an idea of which of the seven values I think the activity most directly addresses. However, it is sometimes difficult to limit the activity to just one value so you may find a couple of topics listed. If you see other values that complement those that I am addressing, feel free to talk about them too. Values overlap so much (such as honesty and integrity) that you might see a need to broaden the activity to include other values also.

Key Words: These are words that will probably come up when you introduce the value. They will certainly be used after the activity during the discussion time. You should know the definition of these words. The definition should be explained at a level your children will understand. Use examples to help explain the words. The first one or two words listed, refer back to the value at the top of the activity. The rest of the words are not listed in any particular order.

Location: This will let you know if you are going to be able to do the activity at your home or if you need to be somewhere special for it to take place.

Time Estimate: I have given you an average time if you did the activity with four people. If you have fewer or greater than four, the time will change accordingly. Also, the ages of the children may affect the amount of time it takes. Notice that I have not included time for discussion in my estimate. This will vary considerably based on the ages of your children. There are a few activities that can not be completed in one session. These activities will be spread out over a few days or weeks. You can do other activities while these continue.

Materials Needed: I have tried to keep the items you will need to a minimum. Hopefully they are things you have around the house or can pick up easily at your local store. Some items need to be saved up over a period of time. To speed up this process, you can ask a neighbor to help you out. Cost has also been taken into consideration. None of the items are very expensive. Be sure that you have enough materials to accommodate all of the participants. Nothing will ruin an activity quicker than running out of materials.

Concept: This is a longer description of the value I feel the activity addresses. It explains the value in greater depth and gives some information about how I am approaching the topic. You can use the information in this section to help you explain the activity to your children and to help guide you when you ask questions after the activity is over. If my concept doesn't agree with your thinking, don't throw out the activity, simply use your own thoughts to introduce it.

Activity: This is a step-by-step description of what will take place. Read through it carefully and visualize each step in your mind. It is best to read through the entire description to get the overall picture before trying to understand each separate step. Once you have the general idea it is easier to see how each step works.

Don't become locked into my activity description. I certainly don't know your individual family well enough to allow for all of the variations that could be done. Since all children develop emotionally, physically and intellectually at different rates, you will have to be the one who decides what will best meet the needs of your family. If as you read through my description of the activity you feel something a little different would work better for your family, make the change. Let my activities become a launching pad for your own creativity.

Important notice: Some of the activities have accompanying illustrations. These illustrations are only to help <u>you</u> better understand how the activity is to be conducted. Do not show the illustrations to your family members. The illustrations showing how to build something such as a tower or a slide are only there to give you a suggestion. This is not the way the tower or slide must, or even should, look. There are a number of solutions to the challenges that have been given. The illustration just shows one possible way that the challenge may be met. Allow your family to solve the challenge using their own thinking and creativity.

You can repeat the activities again in a year or two. Maybe you will want to repeat it in a different place or with a little different twist. Your kids will be older and will have a different perspective during the discussion time.

Discussion Ideas: These are just some questions that you might want to ask. All of the questions tie into the value and concept that are listed at the beginning of the activity outline. It is helpful to read through the questions before doing the activity in order to better understand the purpose of the activity. If you want to address a different topic but still use the activity, simply change the introductory comments that you make before the activity and the discussion questions you use at the end.

I have broken my questions down into three categories. The first set of questions come under the category of "What." This doesn't mean that all the questions start with the word what. Instead, this category means that you are going to ask questions that directly relate to what the activity was about. The questions are used to get the discussion going. They ask about what took place during the activity.

The second set of questions come under the category of "So What." These questions move the discussion from the activity itself to how the activity applies to real life and the value that you are working on. It calls for more thinking on the part of the participants.

The third and last set of questions come under the category of "Now What." These questions reinforce and drive home the message that you want them to take from the activity. They usually ask for a behavior or attitude change. This section is used to make the participants think about their own situation and what they could change or strengthen in their own lives. There are usually only a couple of questions under this category since you are using them to summarize the entire activity.

The length and breadth of the discussion will depend on the ages of your children. All ages can respond to the first set of "What" questions. The "So What" and "Now What" questions could be a little harder for young children. For learning to take place while using activities, it is important to allow them time to reflect on the experience and relate it to their everyday lives. If necessary, you can help them with the more abstract concepts. All of the discussion doesn't have to take place at one time. One advantage you have as a parent is that you don't have a class schedule or a set curriculum that you need to cover. When situations arise later that pertain to the activity, you can reopen the discussion to extend the impact of the activity.

The discussion questions that I have listed are only suggestions. You can use them as they are or skip around and just ask some of them. Adapt them to meet the ages and needs of your children. Have fun with the discussion time. Enjoy each other's comments and don't worry too much about how well you are doing. At the end of the discussion you can make a short summary of what was discussed. You can use this time to reinforce your values message. My only caution is do not turn this into a lecture. Make it short, light and to the point!

One question I get asked often is "Should I participate in the activities or just watch?" I always answer with a resounding "Participate!" My feeling is that the more people you have participating, the more excitement will be generated. If the activity is one where you can join in, do so. If the activity is one where the group is trying to solve a problem, don't be too vocal. Let the kids do the work. Warn other adults who are participating to respect this same rule. Some activities will preclude you from being a part because they need a leader who is outside of the activity. This does not stop other adults from joining in. Just remember that it is the kids that we want to have the experience, so don't allow adults to dominate the activity. As long as you follow that rule, the more the merrier! Another reason to have adults participate is that it gives the activity credibility. When kids see adults participating, then they figure it must not be too bad. For older kids it gives them an excuse to participate. Besides, these are fun activities you will want to be a part of.

Do you want a great way to end your time spent together? Well after the activity has been completed and the discussion is over, join together in a group hug. That's right, gather everyone together and give one big squeeze!

CHAPTER SIX

Helpful Hints to Leading the Discussion Time

What you should do during the discussion itself:

1. Allow for the excitement of the activity to flow over into the discussion.
2. If you have younger children, you will have to explain more and discuss less.
3. Don't embarrass anyone during the discussion time, even to make a joke.
4. Allow for silence. Some questions take longer to think about the answer.
5. Don't let adults dominate the discussion time.
6. Allow people to have different opinions. This is not a court of law where one person is right and the other person is wrong.
7. After someone gives their answer don't say "Great answer." This will make everyone else try to answer with similar thoughts. Just say "Thanks" and continue.

The discussion format I recommended that you use in the previous chapter is:

What? Asking questions related to the activity itself.

So What? Asking questions about what the activity had to do with applications to real life.

Now What? Asking questions that will lead to behavior changes your children can use in their lives.

(There is a longer section on the discussion format in the chapter on "Understanding The Activity Lesson Plan". Two of my other books **Activities That Teach** and **More Activities That Teach** also expand on how to lead a discussion. I don't want to spend too much space here on discussions since there is no need to turn you into expert discussion leaders. These activities will allow you to make an impact in your family without being an expert.)

Questions to Avoid When Leading a Discussion

1. Questions that have a right or wrong answer.
2. Too many questions that can be answered "Yes" or "No."
3. Long, wordy questions where the meaning is forgotten before you even finish asking the question.
4. A question within a question.
5. Questions that have an obvious answer.
6. Questions that are too general or too vague.
7. Questions that your kids do not have enough experience to answer.

Questions That Can Be Used to Keep Your Discussion Going

"Can you give us an example . . ."
"What did you mean when you said . . ."
"What makes you believe that?"
"Please explain what you just said."
"What reason do you have to feel that way?"
"What part of the activity do you base your opinion on?"

"Could you expand on that?"
"What other feelings did you feel?"
"Please tell us more about . . ."
"What did you mean by . . . ?"
"What else can you add?"
"Susan, what do you think about John's answer?"
"Jesse, tell us what you think."
"Well, we have heard from Mindy. Malcom, what do you think?"
"Thanks Armando. Jessica, what do you think?"
"Brandon, you have said a great deal. What do others think?"

When asking these questions, be sure that you do not give the impression that you are asking the individual to defend their answer. You are just seeking further information that would help the discussion.

Activities

Aiming For The Top

KEY WORDS: Perseverance, Goal Setting, Success, Short Term Goal, Long Range Goal

LOCATION: In your home

TIME ESTIMATE: 20 minutes plus discussion time

MATERIALS NEEDED:
- 1 balloon for each participant. The balloon should be about 9 inches in diameter. You can use larger ones, and just not blow them up too much. If the balloons are too small, they won't float well. (Have some extra balloons)
- Masking tape
- 5 paper plates
- A pen or pencil
- A piece of paper
- A ruler

Concept

We want our kids to reach their full potential. One way to help them accomplish that is to teach them to set goals. It has been shown that people who have written well-defined goals have a much better chance of reaching them than people who just wish for happiness, wealth or fame. We want our children to reach for the top of the mountain rather than just settling for whatever comes their way. Some people are willing to settle for a limited amount of success, when with just a little more effort they could achieve a great deal more. This activity will give you a chance to discuss goals and the difference between aiming too low and reaching your full potential.

Activity

Before the activity write "100" points on the first plate, on the second plate write "200" points, "400" on the third, "1,000" on the fourth and "1,500" on the fifth plate. Use masking tape to designate a starting line. Place a short piece of masking tape two feet, three feet, four feet, five feet and six feet from the starting line. The tape will allow you to place the paper plates back in their proper position if they get moved around. Now place a paper plate so that the edge of the plate closest to the starting line is even with the masking tape. The result will be that the closest edge of the plates will be 2, 3, 4, 5 and 6 feet from the starting line. Do not place the paper plates in a straight line. Offset them so that you will know exactly which plate the person is trying to hit. They don't have to be too far apart, six to twelve inches will be enough. To keep the plates from moving around during the activity, tape them to the floor.

You should experiment with the size you want the balloons to be before passing them out. Blow up one of the balloons to the size you think is correct, then hit the balloon with your hand and try to make it land where you want it to. This will give you an idea of how well the particular balloons you purchased will fly before everyone else inflates their balloons. Give each participant a balloon. Have them blow it up to the size you found works best with the particular balloons that you bought and tie it shut. Everyone's balloon should be blown up to about the same size.

Explain that the object of this activity is for each person to hit their balloon with their hand and try to make the balloon come down and make its initial landing on top of one of the plates. The balloon doesn't have to stay on the plate, but it must hit the plate

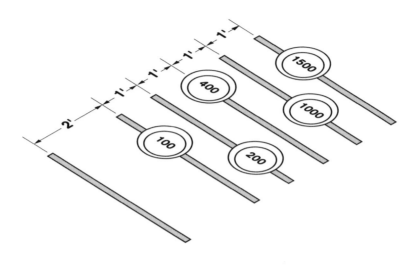

before it hits the floor. Give everyone a few minutes to practice hitting their balloons to get the feel of how far it floats when they hit it.

After some practice to get the feel of the balloons, you are ready to start the contest. One at a time each person will stand at the starting line with their feet and balloon behind the line. Their feet and hands must remain behind the line as they hit the balloon. The hitter will call out which paper plate they are going to aim for and the amount of points that plate is worth before they hit their balloon. They must hit (not throw) the balloon and have it come down on the paper plate they called out. If they do hit the designated plate as the balloon hits the ground, they receive the amount of points marked on the plate. If it hits the proper plate after a bounce, they do not receive any points. If it doesn't hit the plate at all or hits a different plate, they receive no points for that hit.

Each person gets to hit their balloon three times before their turn is over. They may try for the same plate each time or they may change the plate they are aiming for each time they try. Remember, they must call out which plate they are aiming for before each hit.

List each person's name on a piece of paper and record their scores for each round. After all of the participants have taken their three hits, repeat the process for two more rounds. When you have completed, each person will have hit their balloon nine times. The person with the highest score each round is the winner for that round. Keep track of the scores for each round and total them up to get the overall winner.

DISCUSSION IDEAS

"What" Questions
- What was each person's final score?
- Did the same person win each round?
- How hard was it to make the balloon come down where you aimed?
- What strategy did you use to get the balloon to land where you wanted it to?
- Did you get better the more times you hit the balloon?
- Did you tend to choose the high scoring or low scoring plates? Why?
- How did your strategy change as the rounds went on?

"So What" Questions
- Why were the plates that were the farthest away marked with the highest scores?
- How can we compare this activity with goal setting?
- Should we set goals that are easy to reach just so we can say that we reached our goals? Why or why not?
- Which goals give us the most satisfaction when reached, easy or difficult ones? Why?
- How much have you achieved if you set a really hard goal, but only make it part way there?
- How much have you achieved if you set a really simple goal and reach it?

- What can we do if we set a goal and we don't achieve it?
- Can we only be successful if we reach all of our goals?
- If we set a long range goal, why would it be important to set short term goals along the way?

"Now What" Questions

- Would you rather set hard or easy to reach goals? Why?
- What are some of the goals that you wish to achieve in your life?
- How will you measure how successful you are in reaching your goals?

Angels Among Us

KEY WORDS: Caring, Good Deed, Win-Win

LOCATION: At home, school or work

TIME ESTIMATE: Takes place over one week

MATERIALS NEEDED:
- 1 small piece of paper for each participant

Concept

Doing something for other people without expecting anything in return is a valuable trait for each of us to possess. When we do a kind deed for someone else it is a win-win situation. The person who receives the good deed feels good and the person who performed the good deed feels good. When we don't have to worry about getting credit for what we have done it allows us to concentrate on how others feel rather than our own needs and feelings. Our society and family benefits as a whole when people care about each other, when they celebrate each others victories and comfort one another when they are feeling down.

Activity

Call the family together and explain that for one week each person will be the secret pal for someone else in the family. These deeds are to be done without the person you have been assigned knowing who did them. You may enlist the help of others in or out of the family to assist you in completing these good deeds but you are trying to keep your identity a secret from the person to whom you have been assigned. Write each person's name down on a separate piece of paper and have each participant choose one. This person is the one they will do nice things for during the next week

Explain that the purpose of the activity is not for you to buy your secret pal gifts, but rather to do things for them that make them feel good, encourage them or support them in their weekly activities. Some examples would be to make their bed while they were in the bathroom, put a note of encouragement in their lunch, empty the trash can in their room, put a small piece of candy on their pillow before they go to bed, send them a card in the mail, do one of their chores, etc. Everything is to be done secretly. At the end of the week gather the family back together to see if they can guess who their secret pal was.

DISCUSSION IDEAS:

"What" Questions
- Who was your secret pal?
- Were you able to keep the secret from your person?
- What kinds of things were done for you?
- What kinds of things did you do for others?
- Did you get help from others to accomplish any of your good deeds?
- What was the best deed that was done for you?
- What was the deed you enjoyed doing the most?

"So What" Questions
- How did you feel when you discovered what someone had done for you?
- How did you feel when you were doing something for someone else?

- How did you feel as you watched your secret pal discover what you had done for them?
- Was the satisfaction that you received from doing the good deed enough reward?
- How does helping one another show that we care about that person?
- How would our family benefit if we did good deeds for each other more often?
- How would you individually benefit if you did good deeds more often?
- How would society as a whole benefit if people went out of their way to help others without expecting something in return?

"Now What" Questions
- What can we do to help others in our family?
- What can we do to help people outside of our family?

Are You Deaf?

KEY WORDS: Respect, Empathy, Understanding, Handicapped, Impaired, Senior Citizen

LOCATION: At home in front of the television

TIME ESTIMATE: 30 minutes plus discussion time

MATERIALS NEEDED:
- Television
- Optional: A blindfold for each person
- Optional: A VCR

Concept

The saying "Walk a mile in someone else's shoes" could be the theme of this activity. There are many people in this world who have a handicap. It may be something that we can easily see, such as a person in a wheelchair or someone who is blind, or it may be something we can't quickly identify, such as being hard of hearing or diminished eyesight. We need to teach empathy (emotional understanding), not just sympathy (feeling sorry) for people with these problems. The elderly population in the United States is growing at a rapid rate. As people age, some of their senses begin to lose the ability to function properly or completely. Impaired hearing and eyesight are common problems among our elderly population.

Young people have trouble understanding why they need to repeat questions or why some older people lose interest in the conversation when many voices try to talk all at once. It's not that older people aren't interested, it's that they can't hear enough to follow the conversation and they feel embarrassed to keep asking what was said. Respect for the elderly and handicapped is important in any culture. This respect can be fostered by an understanding of their situation.

Activity

Choose a television comedy that your family is not very familiar with. Gather the family in front of the television set. Explain that for the first 15 minutes of the show the sound will be turned off. Everyone will watch the show. During this time discuss among yourselves what you think the show is about. Discuss the story line, the plot, the characters, the setting, etc.

When the show is about half over, have everyone close their eyes. If you would like, give everyone a blindfold to remind them to keep their eyes closed. Another option is to have everyone turn away from the television set so they can't see the screen. Turn the volume back up on the television. You can now hear what is taking place on the show but you won't be able to see the action. Continue to discuss the story line, the plot, the characters, the setting, etc.

Optional: If you have a VCR you can record the show and then watch it normally to see what you missed. This would let you know if you got the story line correct or not.

DISCUSSION IDEAS:

"What" Questions
- How difficult was it to decide what was taking place when you couldn't hear the sound?

- Did people have different ideas about what was taking place?
- How close do you think you came to guessing what was taking place?
- Would you enjoy watching television if you couldn't hear it?
- How difficult was it to decide what was taking place when you couldn't see the picture?
- Did people have different ideas about what was taking place?
- How close do you think you came to guessing what was taking place?
- Would you enjoy watching television if you could only hear it?
- Was it funny with only sound?
- Was it funny with only the picture?

"So What" Questions
- What problems would you have if you were hearing impaired?
- What problems would you have if you were visually impaired?
- Would you feel comfortable watching television with others if you were impaired? Why or why not?
- Would you ask others to explain what was taking place on the television? Why or why not?
- In what other areas would being visually or hearing impaired make life difficult?
- How would the effects of being impaired be different on a young person, a middle aged person, and an older person?
- What are some of the other problems people experience as they grow older?

"Now What" Questions
- How should we treat people who have a handicap or are impaired?
- How can we help people who have a handicap or are impaired?
- How can we show respect to our senior citizens?

Baby Needs

KEY WORDS: Responsibility, Provide, Healthy, Needs, Sexual Activity

LOCATION: In your home

TIME ESTIMATE: 20 minutes plus discussion time

MATERIALS NEEDED:
- 15 - 20 3x5 cards per team of two
- A roll of masking tape (1/2 to 3/4 inches wide)
- A pen or pencil per team of two
- A ruler

Concept

Making a baby is the easiest part of having children. Once the baby is born there are a whole lot of needs that must be met for that baby to grow up healthy and happy. Too many of today's teens are experimenting with sexual activity without realizing the enormous responsibility that comes with having a baby. Discussing the realities of life when you have a baby may help your children decide to wait until they can properly meet the needs of a baby before engaging in sexual activity. This type of discussion is not always easy to have with your kids, but it is a whole lot easier to talk about the topic before a baby is part of the picture rather than after. This activity provides a fairly non-threatening way to begin a discussion.

Activity

Divide into teams of two. If you have an uneven number, one person can work alone. Give each team fifteen to twenty 3x5 cards and a pen or pencil. As one large group, brainstorm what a baby might need during their first year of life. Have <u>each</u> team write the needs mentioned by the group on their 3x5 cards. They should only write one need per card. Here are some examples of needs that a baby could have during their first year: clothes, doctor visits, milk, food, toys, someone to play with them, love, a rocking chair, a car seat, a stroller, a high chair, diapers, baby-sized spoon, blankets, a crib, medicine, story books, a pacifier, baby bottle, shoes, hat, baby powder, a lot of time, etc. As each item is named, comment on why the baby would need this item.

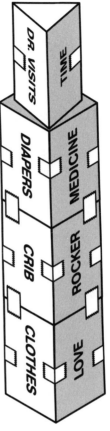

When you have finished naming the items and each team has written them on their cards, you are ready for the next part of the activity. Explain that each team will now use the notecards and masking tape to build a tower. The challenge is to be the team that builds the tallest freestanding tower in ten minutes. Freestanding means that the tower cannot be connected to the ceiling, walls or anything else. They may only use the cards and masking tape. They are not limited in the amount of masking tape they may use. Start by giving each team about twenty four inches of masking tape. If they need more, you may supply it to them. At the end of the designated time, measure the height of each tower to determine the winner.

DISCUSSION IDEAS:

"What" Questions
- How tall was the winning tower?
- How hard was it to think of things a baby would need in their first year?
- How many items did we come up with?
- What was the most unusual item?
- Which items would be most used during the first six months? The second six months?
- Which items are the most expensive? The least expensive?
- Which items would be the easiest to provide? The hardest to provide?

"So What" Questions
- How expensive is a baby during the first year?
- How much time does a baby take during the first year?
- How tiring is it to be the parent of a baby?
- Which of the items that we listed would be hard to provide if you didn't have a lot of money?
- Which items would it be hard to provide if you didn't have a lot of time?
- What would happen to the baby if some of the things they needed were not provided?
- Why isn't just loving a baby enough to have it grow up healthy and happy?
- Why is it hard to be a single parent when the baby is young?
- What happens to a teenager's time after they have a baby?
- What problems would the baby have if the child was born when the parent was still in high school?
- Which items would be hard for a teen parent to provide?
- At what age would you recommend having a baby? Why?
- What other than age are important considerations in deciding when to have a baby?

"Now What" Questions

- Why aren't teenagers ready to meet the needs of babies?
- What can you do to increase the chances of a baby growing up healthy and happy?
- How can you make sure that you don't have a baby when you are too young?

Chain Gang

KEY WORDS: Service to Others, Community, Good Deed

LOCATION: In your community

TIME ESTIMATE: Approximately ten hours over a one week period plus discussion time

MATERIALS NEEDED:
- A piece of paper
- A pen or pencil
- A number of small pieces of paper (about 2 inches by 3 inches)
- Some construction paper
- A pair of scissors
- A stapler or a roll of tape
- A bowl or a jar

Concept

Providing service to others is as rewarding to the individual that performs the service as it is to the recipient of the good deed. We shouldn't think of community service or doing a good deed as work, but rather as a way to pay back those who have helped us. It is our way of repaying the kindness to the nameless people who have helped us, our family or our community. The golden rule says, "Do unto others as you would have them do unto you." This tells us that we shouldn't wait for someone to be kind to us or to the community before we reach out to help others. When we provide a service for the community in general, we don't always receive any reward at all, sometimes not even a thank you. That doesn't make our action any less important. Community service even benefits those who do not join in and help. For example, when we pick up litter along the road everyone in the community benefits.

Activity

Have your family brainstorm good deeds everyone could do to help around the house, to help others and to help the community in general. At this point don't worry how practical the ideas are, just write down everything that comes to mind. Be sure to include things that can be done by the age children you have in your family. Make one list of things that could be done around the house to help each other, such as doing the dishes, taking out the trash or washing the windows, etc. Make a second list of things you could do for other people in the neighborhood or friends such as wash their car, wash their windows, clean up their yard, cut their grass, baby-sit for an evening, etc. Make a third list of community service projects you could undertake either individually or as a family. These don't have to be large projects. They could be as simple as picking up litter, volunteering for an hour at a non-profit organization, helping out a teacher at school, doing something extra at your place of worship, talking with residents at a nursing home, collecting food for your local food bank, etc. Once you have completed the three lists go back over them and cross out the ones that couldn't be done due to time, distance, money, etc.

Write down the ideas that are left on small pieces of paper. Write down only one idea per paper. Count up all of the pieces of paper you have written on. Now use construction paper to construct a paper chain. To do this you cut the construction paper into strips about two inches wide and about five to six inches long. Then make a circle out of the strips by stapling or taping the ends together. Before stapling each piece of paper into a circle, loop it through the previous circle. As you continue this process you will end up with a longer and longer chain of interconnected pieces of paper. Do not have any more circles in the chain than you have pieces of paper with good deeds written on them.

Hang the paper chain up somewhere in the house where everyone will see it. Place the small pieces of paper in a jar or a bowl and place it where everyone will have easy access to it. Now set a time limit, such as a week or two, for the completion of all of the good deeds in the bowl. Explain that during this period everyone in the family should choose good deeds out of the bowl and complete them. Choose a time each day when the family can share which good deeds were completed during that day. For each good deed that was completed, one circle is removed from the paper chain. When the chain is gone, all the good deeds have been accomplished. As a celebration, the entire family should go out for ice cream or something else that you enjoy.

DISCUSSION IDEAS:

"What" Questions
- How hard was it to think up good deeds?
- Which list was the easiest to create? The hardest?
- Which good deeds did you choose to do?
- Which good deed did you enjoy doing the most? The least?
- Which good deeds were done individually? As a group?
- Did we complete all of the good deeds before the deadline?
- Do you think everyone in the family completed the same number of good deeds?

"So What" Questions
- How did you feel when you completed a good deed?
- How did the person you did a good deed for react?
- Did you do the good deed expecting someone to thank you?

- Was it less satisfying to do something for the community instead of an individual? Why or why not?
- Would you do good deeds even if a reward was not promised? Why or why not?
- What would happen if each person did something for someone else every day?
- Why would you do something for people you don't even know?
- Did it bother you that everyone shared equally in the celebration even though everyone didn't work equally? Why or why not?

"Now What" Questions

- How is our community a better place when people do good deeds?
- How do we benefit individually when we help each other without expecting something in return?

Clueless

KEY WORDS: Caring, Individuality, Stereotyping, Unique

LOCATION: In your home

TIME ESTIMATE: 20 minutes plus discussion time

MATERIALS NEEDED:
- 2 pieces of paper for each person
- A pen or pencil for each person

Concept

As family members, we sometimes overlook how unique each person in our family really is. Others think of us as a group such as the Smith's, rather than a collection of individuals who make up a family. When we generalize about groups, we end up thinking in stereotypes based on things we have heard or read. When you think of a football player you think of a big, strong man who can lift small horses over his head. But this isn't true of all football players. Some football players are of average height and weight. You couldn't pick them out in a room full of people. In reality, the more you know about someone the less likely you are to stereotype them. We tend to ignore, fear or make fun of people we don't know much about.

By getting to know people as individuals, we can get past putting a stereotype label on them. You can go to any high school in the country and they will have stereotyped certain people as belonging to groups they have identified as jocks, nerds, stoners, skaters, preppies, etc. This activity gives you a chance to discuss stereotyping and getting to know people as individuals rather than lumping them all together into one group. It also gives you a chance to uncover the uniqueness of the individuals in your family and get to know more about each other.

Activity

Give everyone a piece of paper and something to write with. Have them number one through ten down the paper to create an answer sheet just like they would if they were going to take a test. You will read through the questions listed below. As you read the questions have each person answer them about themselves. Do not let anyone see someone else's answers. When you have gone through all ten questions, have everyone turn their answer sheets face down. You may participate too. Write down your answers after you have read the question aloud.

Now give everyone a second piece of paper. Have them make columns on this piece of paper. They will need one column for each person who is participating, not including themselves. At the top of each column, have them put the name of every person that is going to play. There must only be one name at the top of each column. This paper will now be their second answer sheet.

You will again read through the questions listed below. This time as you read through the questions, have them answer them as they think the other people would have answered that question. They are to write their answers for each person in the appropriately labeled columns. After you have gone through the questions a second time, you are ready to see how many each person got right. Go through each question and have everyone read their answer from the answer sheet they filled out about themselves, then continue to the next question until you have gone through all ten. Each person should keep track on their second answer sheet how many questions they correctly answered for every other person as the answers are being shared. At the end, have each person total up the number of answers they got right about each other. You may have a winner for the most correct answers in each column and an overall winner for the person with the most correct answers in all of the columns.

1. Birthdate (you can include the year, but that makes it really hard)
2. Favorite color
3. Favorite food for dinner
4. Favorite sport to play
5. Favorite television show
6. Favorite type of animal
7. Favorite time to wake up in the morning
8. Place you would most like to visit on a vacation
9. Favorite flavor of ice cream
10. What you like to do for fun

***You can change or add questions to meet specific situations in your family.

DISCUSSION IDEAS:

"What" Questions
- How well did you do?
- Did everyone have the same answers for each question?
- What was the hardest question for you to answer about yourself? The easiest?
- What was the hardest question for you to answer about someone else? The easiest?
- Who was the easiest person to guess the answers for? The hardest person?

- Did you find out something you didn't know before? What was it?
- Were there any answers you would like to hear more about? Which ones?
- Did anybody's answers surprise you? Which ones?

"So What" Questions

- Why didn't everyone answer each question with the same answer?
- What did this quiz tell you about how well you know your family?
- Did you learn anything you didn't know before about someone? What was it?
- How do our likes and dislikes make us individuals?
- What would you have to do when meeting someone before becoming friends?
- When you are friends with someone, how much do you know about them? Explain.
- When we don't know much about a person, is it easy to stereotype them? How about after you get to know them?
- Is stereotyping good or bad? Explain.
- Do all people of a particular race or religion behave the same? Why or why not?

"Now What" Questions

- How can we be individuals even though we all belong to the same family?
- What can we do to make sure we don't stereotype people?

Cookie Time

KEY WORDS: Respect, Laws, Rules, Obey, Consequences

LOCATION: In your home

TIME ESTIMATE: 20 minutes plus discussion and cooking time

MATERIALS NEEDED:
You may use any cookie recipe that you like.

Concept

Everyone needs to respect the laws of their communities. This type of respect extends beyond the criminal law; it also applies to school rules and family rules. Too often we will look at a law or rule and say, "I don't see why that should apply to me." What we don't realize is that we may not be seeing the larger picture. Imagine visiting a gorgeous beach with beautiful white sands and warm inviting water on a warm, sunny day. The water looks very inviting, but there is a sign that says "Beach closed to swimming." As you look around you can't see anything wrong with the water, so in you go. Unfortunately there is a strong undertow current that starts to pull you out to sea. You are barely able to get back to shore safely. The sign forbidding swimming was put there by someone who knew more than you did.

Laws and rules were not created to make life difficult. They were put into place to protect people from harm. Laws and rules also have another purpose. This is to keep everything running smoothly. If people decided that they didn't have to stop at red lights or to drive on the right side of the road, there would be chaos and destruction on the highways. Community laws, school rules and family rules are there to protect us and to provide us with a structure where everyone benefits. Breaking these rules results in consequences that remind us to respect the law and other rules for our own safety and benefit.

Activity

Important notice. I don't want you to waste too many ingredients on cookies that may not even be edible. However, to make the activity really give a strong message you will have to waste a certain amount. So, when doing the first round of the activity you may want to limit the amount of ingredients your kids are allowed to use. Don't influence them too much, but if they want to put in four cups of flour and your recipe only calls for one cup, you may want to say "No you may only use 2 cups." You could also cut the recipe in half before showing it to your kids.

Before bringing your family together, place all of the ingredients and cooking utensils on the table. Do not measure the ingredients out for them, just put the entire container out for them to use. Now bring the family together. Explain that in front of them are all of the ingredients needed to make cookies. Their challenge is to combine the ingredients together to make a batch of cookies without using a recipe. Do not help them! Have them put together all of the ingredients and place the cookies on the cookie sheet ready to bake. Ask them how long and at what temperature they want them baked. Place the cookies in the oven and bake as they instruct.

While the first batch is baking, show everyone the recipe and have them follow the steps as listed. You may help by answering questions this time. When this batch has finished baking, conduct a taste test and check out the difference.

DISCUSSION IDEAS:

"What" Questions
- How many ingredients are needed to make chocolate chip cookies?
- Which ingredient is the most important? The least important?
- How did the order and amount of ingredients you put in when you didn't have the recipe compare with the order and amount that the recipe called for?
- How did the two batches taste?

"So What" Questions
- Why would you want to follow a recipe when baking?
- What is wrong with just "doing your own thing" when it comes to baking?
- How can we compare following a recipe to obeying the law?
- What would happen if everyone made up their own laws?
- What are the consequences of breaking a law?
- What are the consequences when everyone obeys the law?
- How are school rules and family rules different than laws?
- What are the consequences of breaking a school rule? A family rule?
- What are some of the family rules that we have?
- Do you still have to obey a rule that you think is stupid? Why or why not?

"Now What" Questions
- How do laws make our community a better place to live?
- How does having rules benefit our family?
- What would happen if each person could decide which rules they would follow?

Cover Up

KEY WORDS: Honesty, Lying, Truth, Cover Up, Trust

LOCATION: In your home

TIME ESTIMATE: 15 minutes plus discussion time

MATERIALS NEEDED:
- A container (such as a cooking pot or a bucket) that you can put six to eight inches of water in. It should be at least eight inches across
- A quarter
- 10 pennies

Concept

Telling a lie seems simple enough to do. We lie to keep us from getting in trouble, to exaggerate something we did to make ourselves look better, to get others in trouble, to get out of certain situations, etc. However, one of the problems with telling a lie is remembering what we have said. The truth is easy to remember because it really happened. If we make up a lie to meet our needs in a certain situation, then we have to remember what we said later on if someone asks us about it. As we try to cover up our first lie we end up telling more lies. Now our story becomes even more complicated and we have to keep more lies straight. We have to remember what we said to whom and think about who might compare stories with each other. If we don't keep everything straight, someone will catch us in our lie and expose the truth. Rather than spend a lot of time and energy trying to cover up our first lie with other lies, wouldn't it be easier to just tell the truth? Once you have a reputation as a liar it is hard to get people to trust you. Trust is hard to get back once you have lost it.

Activity

Fill a container with six to eight inches of water. Begin the activity by placing a quarter on the bottom of the container right in the middle. Give the first person ten pennies. Explain that their challenge is to cover up the quarter with the pennies. The pennies must be dropped one at a time from a height of two inches above the water. After they have dropped all ten pennies, count how many pennies landed and stayed on the quarter. Estimate what percentage of the quarter they covered. Retrieve the pennies and let the next person have their turn. When everyone has taken a turn, repeat the process again to see if they can improve.

DISCUSSION IDEAS:

"What" Questions
- How well did you do covering the quarter?
- How many pennies did you get to land on the quarter?
- How easy was it to get the pennies to land on the quarter?
- What techniques did you use?
- How successful were these techniques?

"So What" Questions

- How can we compare this activity to trying to cover up a lie that we told?
- Do you sometimes have to tell more than one lie to cover up the first lie? Why or why not?
- How hard is it to remember which lies you told to which person? Explain.
- How can we keep from having to tell more lies to cover up the first one?
- How much control do we have over others passing on our lies?
- Describe a situation where someone may have to tell more lies after they told the first lie.
- What happens when someone catches you in a lie?
- How easy is it to convince someone you are telling the truth after they have caught you lying?
- How can you get that person to trust you again?

"Now What" Questions

- Why is telling the truth easier than lying even if the truth may get us in trouble?
- How does being honest help people trust us?

Dessert First

KEY WORDS: Responsibility, Creativity

LOCATION: In your home during dinner

TIME ESTIMATE: 40 minutes plus discussion time

MATERIALS NEEDED:
- Dinner with a number of courses
- Two sheets of paper
- Two pens or pencils

Concept

A friend of mine from Colorado by the name of Don Shaw told a story about a second grade teacher who instructed the class to draw a picture of an ocean and a boat for their art project. One boy finished much earlier than the rest of the class. The teacher went over and saw that he had only drawn the ocean with no boat. She said, "I only see the ocean. Where is your boat?" The young boy replied, "It sank." The teacher didn't know whether to give the boy an "F" for not completing the assignment or an "A" for creativity.

Our society is looking for creative people in every field. Creativity is not something that someone has to be born with; it can be learned. Many times creativity is simply allowing yourself to look at things differently or to ask the questions "What if?" and "Why not?" It also means to stop listening to those who say, "We do it that way because it has always been done that way." Use this activity to help your children begin to look at things in a different way and to start thinking outside the ordinary. The skill of creativity can be learned, and it is up to each person to pursue this skill.

Activity

This activity takes place at the dinner table. Instead of serving your food courses in their normal order, everything is served in the reverse order. You start out by giving everyone dessert. Do not bring out the next course until dessert has been eaten. Then bring on the main course. Next bring out the rolls. Next bring out the soup and last bring out the salad.

After dinner, divide your family into two groups. Each group gets a piece of paper and something to write with. The challenge is to think up as many ways as possible to improve a bathtub. This could include such things as putting a television set in the wall above the tub, making the sides of the tub clear and using them as a fish tank, making the bottom of the tub out of rubber so it is soft, having a built in pillow, etc. Cost is not an issue. Send the two groups into different rooms so they can't hear each other discuss. Give them a set amount of time such as ten to fifteen minutes to make their list. Explain that the team with the longest list will be the winner. You can also give recognition to the team with the most creative or unique improvement. After time has been called, bring the teams together and have them share their lists.

Take the process one step further with this question: "Now that we have heard each team's ideas, what great ideas can we come up with all together?" Brainstorm for a few minutes.

DISCUSSION IDEAS:

"What" Questions
- How did you like having dessert first?
- Did the food taste the same?
- How strange was it to eat dinner backwards?
- How did your team do creating improvements for the bathtub?
- Were improvements hard to think up?
- Did it get any easier the more you thought about it?
- Which were easier to come up with, the first three or the last three improvements? Why?
- As a whole were your team's suggestions practical or off the wall?
- How did we do as one large group coming up with suggestions?

"So What" Questions
- How hard is it to change the way we normally do things?
- How often do you think about why we do things the way we do?
- How hard do you think it would be to invent new things?
- How hard do you think it would be to improve things that were already invented?
- Do you think some people are more creative than others?
- Can creativity be learned?
- Why is creativity valuable?
- Do you think of yourself as a creative person? Why or why not?
- Name something creative you have done.
- What are some jobs that require very little creativity? A lot of creativity?

"Now What" Questions
- How do we measure creativity?
- Should we let others judge how creative we are?
- What could you do to become more creative?

Drug Concentration

KEY WORDS: Responsibility, Alcohol, Tobacco, Drugs, Peer Pressure

LOCATION: In your home

TIME ESTIMATE: 20 minutes plus discussion time

MATERIALS NEEDED:
- 40 3x5 cards
- A pen or pencil for each person
- A piece of paper for each person
- A dice

Concept

Alcohol, tobacco and other illegal drugs are all harmful to our children and youth. While alcohol and tobacco are legal for adults, they are illegal for underage users. These laws are due to the increased risk that younger people have of addiction and other adverse reactions. Drugs such as cocaine, PCP, marijuana, heroin, inhalants, etc. are troublesome to those of all ages. I will use the term drugs to refer to alcohol, tobacco and other drugs.

Your children probably already receive drug education at school. This activity gives you a chance to discuss this information with your children and make your own statements regarding their acceptance in your family. You can also take the opportunity to talk about the fact that if your children hang around with people who use drugs, it increases the chance that they will try drugs.

Research has shown that if parents take the time to discuss substance abuse with their children, the likelihood that their children will use illegal drugs goes down. We also know from advertising research that repetition of information allows us to remember the information longer. This activity allows both of these reinforcements to take place.

If you need drug information, your school or local library will be glad to supply you with what you need.

Activity

This activity plays like the game of Concentration. You will lay pairs of cards face down on the floor or table, and the participants will try to match them up. To begin, have everyone help you create the cards. By helping to write the drug facts on the cards, the information is already beginning to be reinforced. You can use the drug facts found at the end of this activity or have your children write down information they have learned at school or elsewhere. Each fact will have to be written on two separate 3x5 cards.

Once the facts have been written on the cards, arrange them face down on the floor or table. You can arrange them in rows or just randomly lay them down. To begin the activity have each person roll the dice. The person rolling the highest number goes first, and then take turns starting with the person on the left of the highest roller. The object is to match the highest number of drug fact cards.

Before each turn, have the player roll the dice to determine how many points a match will be worth. For example, if they roll a five and then find a match, they receive five points. Each turn lasts only one try. Have the player turn over one card and read aloud the drug fact written on the card. Then when they choose a second card to turn over, they must read the fact written on that card also, whether it is a match or not. Remember, we are trying to reinforce the facts through repetition. Even if they correctly match up two cards, their turn is over. If a correct match is made, put both cards on top of each other and leave them face up on the floor or table. This allows the cards to read by the other players as they wait for their turn, once again reinforcing the drug fact. The person with the highest score after all of the cards have been matched is the winner. Have each person keep their own score.

Drug Facts:

1. Alcohol is more dangerous for young people than it is for adults because their bodies haven't stopped growing.
2. Smoking marijuana is more dangerous today than it was in the 1960's because the THC content is stronger.
3. Marijuana can cause lung cancer just like tobacco does.
4. Marijuana stays in your body for up to 30 days.
5. Inhalants affect the central nervous system and can cause damage to the brain and the lungs, as well as cause death.
6. Cocaine use can cause addiction with only a couple of uses.
7. Marijuana can produce distortions of hearing, vision and your sense of time.
8. The most common cancer caused by smoking tobacco is lung cancer.
9. The addictive drug found in tobacco is nicotine.
10. Any use of drugs during pregnancy without a doctor's prescription may be harmful to the unborn child.
11. The most commonly abused drug in the United States is alcohol.
12. Alcohol is the leading cause of automobile deaths in the United States.
13. Drug dealers mix substances like sugar and baby powder with certain drugs to make more money.
14. Alcohol can cause harm to your liver.
15. The younger you are, the easier it is to become addicted to a drug.

16. Kids usually get drugs from their friends rather than from drug dealers.
17. Most smokers start before the age of nineteen.
18. Most smokers wish they could quit.
19. When you drink too much alcohol you destroy brain cells.
20. Peer pressure is one reason many teens give for using drugs.

DISCUSSION IDEAS:

"What" Questions
- How hard was it to match the cards?
- What did rolling the dice add to the game?
- Which fact did you find most interesting? Least interesting?
- How many of these facts did you know before today?
- Where did you learn those facts?

"So What" Questions
- What effect can drugs have on your body?
- Why would drugs affect people under twenty one more than someone over twenty one?
- How would using drugs affect your schoolwork?
- How would using drugs affect someone who had a job?
- How does drug use hurt our country?
- Why do we encourage kids to not use drugs?
- Can other people make you use drugs? Why or why not?
- How do the friends we choose help influence whether we will use drugs or not?

"Now What" Questions
- What reasons would you give for not using drugs?
- Why should we choose our friends carefully?

Earth Detectives

KEY WORDS: Respect, Responsibility, Environment

LOCATION: Outdoors where you can dig in the dirt. Any area will do, but a place that has had moisture recently will add to the excitement since there will be more things to observe. Likely locations could be your backyard, garden area, flower bed or at the edge of a river, pond or lake.

TIME ESTIMATE: 15 minutes plus discussion time

MATERIALS NEEDED:
- You will need one set of these items for each person or team of two :
- A string four feet long
- A spoon (that you don't mind being used for digging) or small trowel
- A piece of paper
- A pen or pencil

Concept

We all know that this is the only earth we will ever have. Taking care of it is each generation's responsibility. However, we usually think of caring for the environment on such a large scale that we forget that the environment is all around us. Your children might not be the ones to save the whales or clean up the air, but they can respect the area in which they live. Respecting the environment is just one part of respecting the community where we live. This activity will allow you to talk about the importance of respecting the environment and the impact that nature has on our lives.

Activity

For this activity I would suggest that you have your family work individually or in teams of two. If you have more than two people looking at one spot, someone becomes a passive observer instead of an active participant. Each person or team of two can work in their own area and then compare results after they finish.

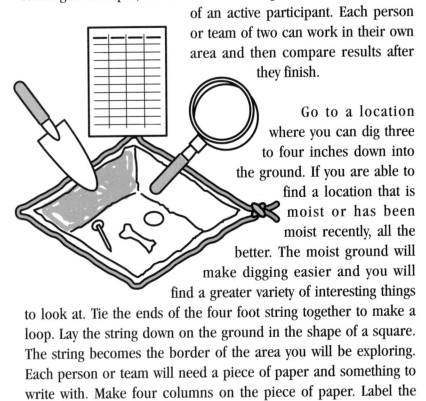

Go to a location where you can dig three to four inches down into the ground. If you are able to find a location that is moist or has been moist recently, all the better. The moist ground will make digging easier and you will find a greater variety of interesting things to look at. Tie the ends of the four foot string together to make a loop. Lay the string down on the ground in the shape of a square. The string becomes the border of the area you will be exploring. Each person or team will need a piece of paper and something to write with. Make four columns on the piece of paper. Label the columns "Animals," "Plants," "Minerals" and "Other."

Now begin to explore your designated piece of ground. Write on the paper everything you observe. Place each item in one of the four categories on your paper. Once you have listed everything on the surface of the ground begin to dig below the surface. Go down about one inch and repeat your observations, once again listing everything you see. Continue this until you have gone down three to four inches into the soil. Each layer will have a variety of objects for you to list. Try to list as many items as you can. You can set up a challenge between teams by seeing who can list the most items in each category. If you are going to set up a challenge, then a time limit should be set. A 10 to 15 minute time limit is reasonable in most locations. If you have a magnifying glass, the items you find can be studied in greater detail. Be sure that if one team has found something really unusual that all the teams get a chance to take a look. If you have set a time limit, simply call a "time out" and allow everyone to observe. If you would like to repeat the activity, move to a different location and start all over again.

Discussion Ideas:

"What" Questions

- How hard was the ground to dig in?
- How many items in each category did you find?
- What category was the easiest to find things in? Why do you think this was true?
- What category was the hardest to find things in? Why do you think this was true?
- How did what you observed change as you moved deeper into the ground?
- What was the most unusual thing you found? The most common?
- Did you find anything that is not normally found in the ground?
- What was one thing that you really enjoyed looking at?
- If you looked at more than one location, was there any difference in what you observed between the two locations?

"So What" Questions

- Did you find more or less than you expected to?
- What impact had humans had on the ground you observed?

- Why are insects important to us?
- Why are plants important to us?
- What would happen if all of the plants died?
- What would happen if all of the insects died?
- How important is the environment to us?
- What does it mean to respect the environment?
- What would happen if everyone respected the environment? What if no one did?

"Now What" Questions
- How should we treat the environment?
- Who is responsible to help protect the environment?
- What can each one of us do to help respect the environment?
- What can we do as a family to help respect the environment?

The idea for this activity was suggested to me by Dwayne Evans. Thanks Dwayne!

Eat What You Earn

KEY WORDS: Perseverance, Work Ethic, Benefits

LOCATION: In your home

TIME ESTIMATE: 15 minutes during a family meeting and then one week to complete the activity. At the end of the week you will have a dinner.

MATERIALS NEEDED:
- A list of jobs or responsibilities that you would like done around the house
- A points earned chart
- A fancy dinner with dessert

Concept

The work ethic is a tough one to teach because most of your children are too young to have jobs. You could discuss the value of work in relation to their schoolwork and grades, but that doesn't seem to have the impact that it once did. This activity can show a direct correlation between how much work you do and the resulting benefit that this effort can bring. More importantly, it can show the opposite. The activity can show that if you do not work hard, you will be missing out on certain benefits.

Activity

This activity starts with a family meeting. At the meeting you will explain that at the end of one week you are going to serve a fancy meal and then take the family out for dessert. (If going out for dessert causes a problem, you can substitute a special dessert at home.) However, there is one catch to this dinner: each person must earn what they eat! You will have to have a menu already prepared as to what you are going to serve at the dinner. This list should be written on a large piece of paper that you can post on the wall later. The list should start with the plate, silverwear, glasses, napkin, etc. Then go on to list the food itself. Make sure that there are a number of different items. Try to make the meal appealing to your children. You can have more than one main course if different kids love different items, or maybe a variety of side dishes that they love. Don't worry about how normal the meal looks; just make sure that your kids will want to eat it. Then have something really special for dessert, or better yet, have a variety of great choices for dessert.

Now that you have their mouths watering and their attention, it is time for you to reveal that everything on your list comes with a price tag. On the paper with the menu, list the cost of each item. Don't use dollar amounts because the kids will get caught up in arguing about how much each item is worth. Instead just assign points to each item. For example, a plate may be worth 50 points, a fork 25 points, a glass 40 points, one helping of meat 200 points, one dinner roll 25 points, mashed potatoes 100 points, gravy 50 points, a slice of pizza 200 points, pudding 75 points, ice cream 300 points, apple pie 200 points, etc.

Once you have shown them the menu and the cost of each item, it is time to show them the jobs and responsibilities list. Responsibilities are things that they probably already do such as make their bed, wash the dishes and do their homework before watching television. Jobs are the extra things that you would like done. For example, clean their room, wash a certain number of windows, dust, sweep the garage, wash the car, vacuum the inside of the car, do a load of laundry, change a bed, clean the bathroom, pull weeds, give the dog a bath, etc. Once again, this list of jobs needs to be written down on a large piece of paper so it can be posted throughout the week.

Next to each job you will write down how many points that job is worth. Compare the points that they can earn with the points you are charging for the food. You want to be sure that they can actually earn the number of points it will take to eat a great meal. Make the less desirable or time consuming jobs worth more points than the easy ones. Also on the list you will need to indicate how often this particular job can be done. For example, making their bed can be done once a day. You wouldn't give points for it twice in one day just because they took their bed apart. The car probably only needs washed or vacuumed once during the week. Be sure there are plenty of jobs for your kids to choose from.

You will need to make one more chart. This one will be for keeping a record of which jobs each child has done and how many points it was worth. At the end of the week, total up the points for each person. This tells them how many points they will have to spend when the big meal is served. There are also rules about how they spend their points. Just like you don't get a choice about paying taxes or bills like trash and sewer service, they don't get any choice about having to first buy their utensils to use while eating their meal. Also just like in real life, they can't spend all of their points on dessert. You have to be sure everyone has clothes to wear and there is gas in the car before you can spend your money on the fun things in life. You can decide what are the required choices. For example, you could require them to buy one vegetable, one or two side dishes and one main course in addition to their eating utensils. Then, however many points they have left can be spent on desserts.

Make a big production out of the night of the big meal. If you really want to play it up, you can create some play money that represents the points they have earned. Then have them pay you as they receive each item. This really helps to drive the point home. The rules of the activity require everyone to stay at the dinner table from the start all the way through dessert, even if they have run out of points. This helps to point out that those who worked hard receive a benefit, while those that didn't work as hard get less out of life.

DISCUSSION IDEAS:

The discussion for this activity does not take place until after the dinner is over.

"What" Questions
- How many points did you earn?
- What jobs did you choose to complete?
- Did you choose to do a lot of little jobs or did you choose just a few high point jobs? Why?
- How did you feel when you had to pay for your plate, drinking glass and utensils?
- Did you have enough points?
- If you ran out of points, how did you feel?
- Would you have purchased more food if you had earned more points?

"So What" Questions
- What must we do to earn money in our society?
- How does this activity compare with having a job?
- Are all jobs worth the same amount of money? Why not?
- What essentials do we have to spend our money on?
- What kinds of things are up to us as to whether we buy them or not?

- What happens in real life when we run out of money?
- Money can't buy happiness, but what does it buy?
- Is hard work rewarded in our country? Explain.
- How does having a good education allow you to have more money?
- If you don't work, what happens to your ability to buy things?
- If you don't work hard, what happens to you on your job?

"Now What" Questions
- Why is working hard valued in our society?
- What are the benefits of hard work?
- What happens if we quit trying to do something just because it is hard to do?

Family Encyclopedia

KEY WORDS: Caring, Bonding, Memories

LOCATION: In your home

TIME ESTIMATE: 20 minutes plus discussion time

MATERIALS NEEDED:
- Questions written on 3x5 cards
- Masking tape
- Paper and a pen or pencil
- 1 dice or a deck of cards

Concept

Family bonding comes from sharing experiences and memories with each other. It is this sharing that gives us a common background that we can draw upon to get us through hard times, to make us more aware of how special our family is and to set us apart as a unit from the rest of the world. We need to foster the idea of "one for all and all for one" by reinforcing our knowledge of each other and what we have in common.

Activity

You will need to spend some time working on this activity before your family sits down to play it. This activity is loosely based on the television show "Jeopardy." You will need to create five questions for each of five different categories that relate to your family. Some suggested categories might be "Birthdays," "Trips," "Places We've Lived," "Happenings," "Individuals," "Pets," "Favorite Foods," etc.

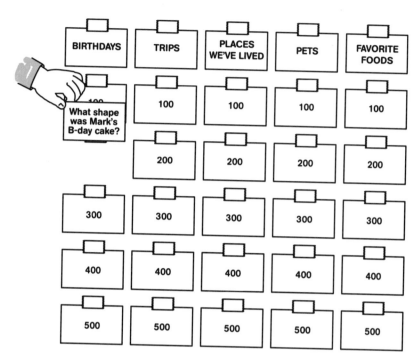

Remember, you will need to have five questions for each category.

Here are some examples of the kinds of questions you can use. Birthdays: What is Tom's birthday? What was one present that Maria received on her last birthday? Where did we celebrate Jackie's birthday two years ago? Trips: Where did we go last year that involved water? How many times have we visited the mountains in the last two years? Where is our favorite place to go on a Saturday? Happenings: What sports team did Maria play for three years ago? Who in our family has had a broken bone? When did we buy our last car? Individuals: What in Tom's favorite color? What was Maria's grade point average last semester? What is Dad's favorite sport? What is one of Mom's hobbies? As you can see from these examples, there is a wide variety of questions that you can fit under any one category.

Now that you have five categories and five questions in each category, you are ready to set up the game. On five of the cards, print the five categories that you have chosen. On the other cards, write each of the questions you have created. Now choose a place where you are going to play this game. Use the masking tape to put the cards with the five categories written on them up on the wall. Now tape the cards with questions on the wall under their proper categories. Tape the questions with the words facing the wall so no one can see what the questions are. Put the easy questions at the top of the column right under the card with the category and put the questions that are harder to answer lower in the column. When you are finished setting the game up, you will have five columns with six cards in each column going down the wall. At the top of each column will be the category and under each category will be five cards with the questions turned towards the wall. Now on the cards that are turned towards the wall, you need to put point totals. Each question is worth a different number of points. On the first card that is right under the category, write 100 points. On the next one write 200 points. Continue down the column adding 100 each time until you reach the last one which will be 500 points. Do this same thing to each category.

You are now ready to start the game. You can roll a dice or cut a deck of cards to see who is going to go first, second and so on. The first person chooses a category and decides which question they wish to try. They do not need to go in order down any of the categories. They may skip around and choose any category and any point value they wish. When they choose the card that they want to answer, then you turn that card over and read the question out loud. If they get the answer right, then they receive the points that were on the card. If they do not answer the question correctly, then they lose the number of points that were on the card. In addition, if they are wrong then the person whose turn it is next has the opportunity to answer the question. If the next person does not want to try to answer the question, they may pass. Each person, in order, may try to answer the question, but if they attempt it and they are wrong, then they also lose the points.

When everyone has tried to answer the question that wants to, then play goes back to the person who was next after the player that originally got the question wrong. If the original player gets the correct answer then they get another turn. However, they can only get two turns in a row even if they get both of the questions correct before play passes on to the next person. When each question is over, tape it back on the wall in the same spot with the question now showing. This will remind everyone of the questions that have been asked. You play until all of the questions have been answered. High score wins the game.

Variation: Have family members make up questions to go in each of the categories that you have decided upon. They can still play since the questions will be turned face down on the wall so they won't know which questions they made up. Another option would be for each person to make up questions for one category and then have to choose from the other categories. That way they wouldn't accidentally get their own question.

Discussion Ideas:

"What" Questions
- Which categories did you find to be the easiest? The hardest?
- Which question was the easiest for you to answer? The hardest?
- Which question do you wish you would have gotten to answer?
- Which question are you glad you didn't have to answer?

"So What" Questions
- What does this game show us about how well we know our family and its history?

- How does knowing our family history help us bond together as a family?
- Why is bonding together something we would want to do?
- What are other ways that families can bond together?
- How would bonding together help us when we are going through troubled times?
- Why are memories important to have as a family?

"Now What" Questions
- What specific things can we do to help bond our family together?

Friends

KEY WORDS: Caring, Friendship, Qualities, Positive, Negative, Influence

LOCATION: In your home

TIME ESTIMATE: 20 minutes plus discussion time

MATERIALS NEEDED:
- 5 sheets of 8 ½ by 11 paper
- A sheet of paper to keep score on
- A pen or pencil
- Masking tape
- A pair of scissors
- A ruler
- 1 rubber band per person

Concept

Friendship is something that we all value. Friends fall into two categories. The first category is our really close friends, those who we share our feelings and thoughts with. The second category are those we spend time with because we share a class together at school or an interest such as sports or a hobby. We choose our friends for a variety of reasons. They may have qualities such as they make us laugh, make us feel good, share our likes and dislikes, listen well, care about how we feel, like the same things we do or are trustworthy. The friends we choose have a major impact on our lives. Many times the people we hang around with have an influence on our thinking and behavior. Therefore, we need to be careful about who we choose to be our friends.

It takes two people to make a friendship. The other side of having friends is being a friend. Are we the kind of person others would want to hang out with? Do we possess the qualities that make others want to spend time with us? Having a friend means being a friend.

Activity

Cut each of the five sheets of paper into fourths. You will end up with twenty pieces of paper 4¼ inches by 5½ inches. Number each piece of paper using the numbers one through twenty. As a family, brainstorm different qualities that you would want in a friend and that you would not want in a friend. Each time the group settles on a positive or negative description, write it down on one of the pieces of paper on the opposite side from the number. Put only one quality on each piece of paper. It is best if you end up with an equal number of positive and negative qualities.

Once you have written a positive or negative description on each sheet of paper, it is time to group the descriptions. You will place each of the descriptions into one of four groups. The first group is those descriptions that you must have in a friend. The second group is those descriptions which you would like to have in a friend. The third group is those descriptions which you would not like to have in a friend, and the fourth group is those descriptions which you must not have in a friend. As a family, decide which group each of your descriptions should be placed into. If you can't come to an agreement on the proper group, then a majority vote makes the decision. Once they are in the chosen groups, it is time to add points to each description. Please write the following point designations on each piece of paper on the same side as you wrote the qualities. Descriptions in the "must have" group are worth ten

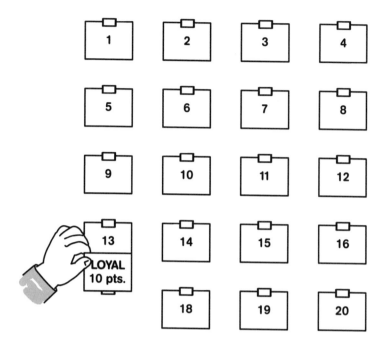

points. Descriptions in the "would like to have" group are worth five points. Descriptions in the "would not like to have" group are worth minus five points. Descriptions in the "must not have" group are worth minus ten points.

Now choose a large empty space such as a wall or the back of a door. Use masking tape to tape the qualities up on the wall. Only the numbers (1-20) should be showing. They should be randomly placed with about three inches between each piece of paper. Make a line on the floor with the masking tape about nine feet from the wall. This distance can be adjusted depending upon the age of your kids, but don't make it too easy. Have each person stand behind the line and shoot their rubber band at the pieces of paper. Everyone rotates taking one shot at a time. Keep track of which pieces of paper they hit (using the numbers which are visible) on a separate piece of paper. If anyone does not hit five pieces of paper with their first five shots, allow them to continue shooting until they have five numbers written down. Do not turn any of the pieces of paper over until everyone has finished. When everyone has finished, turn the pieces of paper over and record the scores of each person. Add up the positive and negative numbers on the papers they hit to arrive at their score. Some of the scores may end up as a minus number.

Now tape the papers back up on the wall, except this time put them face up (with the qualities showing). Once again repeat the same steps as above. Since you will be able to see the positive and negative numbers assigned to each quality, you can keep score as the shooting is taking place.

DISCUSSION IDEAS:

"What" Questions
- How hard was it to think of positive descriptions? Negative descriptions?
- How hard was it to place them in the various groups?
- Was there agreement among the family on the descriptions and placement?
- How well were you able to hit the paper that you were aiming for?
- What was your score when the papers were placed face down? Face up?

"So What" Questions
- Would you pick your friends without knowing them first? Why or why not?
- How long does it take for you to get to know someone?
- How do we get to know someone?
- What is the difference between a close friend and someone we just hang out with?

- What is the positive description that is most important to you when choosing a friend?
- What is the negative description that is most important for you to avoid when choosing a friend?
- How do your friends influence what you think?
- How do your friends influence how you behave?
- Can you describe a situation where someone you know started hanging out with the wrong crowd and suffered because of it?

"Now What" Questions

- Why is it important to choose our friends carefully?
- Which of the positive descriptions of friendship that we listed do you offer as a friend to others?

Golden Gate Bridge

KEY WORDS: Cooperation, Responsibility, Compromise, Teamwork, Problem Solving,

LOCATION: In your home

TIME ESTIMATE: 15 minutes plus discussion time

MATERIALS NEEDED:
- 1 bag of miniature marshmallows (You will use about 60 per team)
- 75 round wooden toothpicks per team of two, plus some extra
- A soup can for each team (teams can share if necessary)
- A ruler

Concept

Our society places a lot of emphasis on being a self sufficient individual that can deal with any and all problems without the help of others. In reality, this is not the best way to get some things accomplished. Sure we need to be independent thinkers and be personally responsible for our own actions, but in many cases we can actually accomplish more when we team up and work together.

Many of today's businesses have recognized the value of working together in teams. The problem with this is that much of our educational system is based on working independently. Working in teams or in groups in the school setting has some problems, such as grading. Since the workplace is concerned with producing a product or service and doesn't give out grades, they can easily use the team approach to improve their productivity and profitability. Cooperation, compromise, teamwork and problem solving are all topics which our children and youth need to explore. However, cooperation does not take away our own personal responsibility to perform to the best of our ability or to contribute to the end product.

Activity

Divide your group into teams of two. Give each team about 60 marshmallows and 75 toothpicks. Prepare the marshmallows ahead of time by leaving them out of the bag for about an hour. This will allow then to harden slightly and make them easier to work with. Explain to your family that their challenge is to build the longest bridge that they can. The bridge must be high enough off of the ground, for its entire length, that a soup can is able to pass underneath it the short way. In other words, you must be able to push the round end of the can under and through the bridge between the braces or supports along its length. In building the bridge, the teams may use as many toothpick supports as they wish as long as the soup can is still able to pass under the bridge. The bridge must also be at least one toothpick wide at the top. The teams may use the soup can while they are building their bridge to be sure it is high enough. If a team runs out of marshmallows or toothpicks, you can allow them to get more.

Allow about twelve minutes for the teams to complete their bridges. However, for the first sixty seconds of their building time they cannot touch either the marshmallows or the toothpicks. During this time all they are allowed to do is to talk about their plans for building the bridge. Remind them that the winner will be the team that has the longest bridge. Explain that it will be the length of the top of the bridge that you will measure, not the

bottom. Count down the twelve minutes of building time for them as they work so they will know how much time they have left. With two minutes to go, surprise them with this announcement, "You have two minutes of building time left, but from now on there can be no talking. All work must be done in complete silence." When time has expired, use a ruler to determine the winner.

Variation: To make the activity more difficult, require that only one person on the team handle the marshmallows and the other team member handle the toothpicks. This variation requires them to use a lot more cooperation. If you use this variation, give them fifteen minutes to build the bridge.

DISCUSSION IDEAS:

"What" Questions
- How long was each bridge?
- How well did you use your sixty seconds of planning time?
- Did you follow your plan? Why or why not?
- If you made changes, what were they?
- Did you look at the other teams' bridges to get ideas?
- Did both members of the team contribute equally to the plan? In the building?
- Did the time left have any influence on how fast you worked?

- How did having to work in silence affect your ability to build?
- If you were to repeat this activity, what would you do differently?

"So What" Questions

- How easy was it for both of you to agree on the bridge design?
- Is it O.K. to get ideas from other teams?
- How is working together different from working alone?
- What are the advantages of working together? The disadvantages?
- What is meant by the phrase "Two heads are better than one"?
- How does our behavior change as we get closer to a deadline?
- How does this activity show cooperation?
- Do we have less responsibility for a project when we work with someone? Why or why not?

"Now What" Questions

- How does cooperation help us when working to solve a problem?
- What can you do to be more cooperative when working with others?

Gotcha

KEY WORDS: Honesty, Trust

LOCATION: In your home

TIME ESTIMATE: 20 minutes plus discussion time

MATERIALS NEEDED:
- A game that uses a board on which the action takes place, such as Monopoly

Concept

Do we only call what we do cheating or dishonest if someone catches us? If you cheat just a little bit but no one notices or cares, is that O.K.? Why do we have rules or laws in school and in our community? You see, how we behave when no one is looking depends on how honest we really are. Without others being able to trust us, then our family and society will break down. Our relationships with each other depend on trust which comes from being truthful and honest in both our speech and our behavior, even when no one is watching us.

Activity

Set the board game up just as you normally would. All the rules of the game are still in force. However, you are going to add a twist to the game. One person is designated as "it." Play the game as you normally would. At any point during the next three to five minutes, the person who was designated as "it" calls out the phrase "Gotcha." Everyone else must immediately close their eyes and cover them with their hands for fifteen seconds. All the players must count in unison out loud for fifteen seconds. (The best way to make sure the proper time is allowed is to have them say a word after each number such as "One Mississippi" or "One boxcar," etc.)

During this fifteen second time period, the person who is "it" now has the opportunity to change the playing board around. "It" may rearrange up to three items. These changes could be with the playing pieces, the money or cards, improving their position or making someone else have a worse position. "It" also has the choice of moving his hands around the playing board, but not moving or changing anything. At the end of the fifteen seconds everyone opens their eyes. Their challenge is to work as a group to recognize any changes on the board and move everything back where it belongs. If they get everything back to the original place then the player who made the moves loses their next turn. If they do not get everything back where it belongs, the items that they didn't notice stay where they were moved and the player who was "it" gets to have an extra turn. The player who was "it" must reveal what items they missed.

The game now continues where you left off. The person to the left of "it" now becomes "it." Continue repeating this process until everyone has had two or three chances to be "it." You as the leader can decide how much time should pass before you stop the game again so that the next "it" can make his or her changes. Once everyone has had enough chances to be "it" you can end the game.

DISCUSSION IDEAS:

"What" Questions
- What kinds of things were changed?
- How hard was it to decide what to change?
- Which things were the easiest to notice?

- Which things were the hardest to notice?
- Did anyone choose not to move anything around? Why or why not?

"So What" Questions

- How did the moving of things around disrupt the flow of the game?
- How did having to concentrate on the board change the way you played the game?
- Did having the opportunity to cheat make the game more or less fun? Why?
- How did you feel when you knew someone else was having the opportunity to cheat?
- How does knowing a person has cheated affect how much you trust them?
- How hard is it to trust someone who has treated you dishonestly in the past?
- Describe some situations where you can either be honest or not. Examples: The clerk at the store gives you too much change; A lamp is broken while you and the dog are the only ones home; A lot of people have been in and out of the kitchen when Mom finds out someone ate the cookies she made for a party, etc.
- How does honesty affect trust?
- What happens when you don't trust someone?
- How hard is it to get trust back from someone after you have lost it?

"Now What" Questions

- What are the benefits to being known as an honest person?
- How is trust built between people?
- Explain this phrase "The real test of honesty is what you do when no one is looking or will ever find out what you did."

Hands

KEY WORDS: Cooperation, Working Together, Competition

LOCATION: In your home

TIME ESTIMATE: 15 minutes plus discussion time

MATERIALS NEEDED:
- A jar of peanut butter
- A jar of jelly
- A table knife for each person
- Two pieces of bread per person

Concept

Many times we try to accomplish tasks by ourselves instead of working together. Most jobs would be completed faster, easier and with less effort if we cooperated with each other. There are times when we need to compete and times when we need to work together. Knowing when to compete and when to cooperate, will help each of us succeed in today's society. Some people believe that asking for help is a sign of weakness. The truth is that asking for help when you need it and working together on a project is an example of working smarter, rather than harder.

Activity

Begin by giving each person one piece of bread and a table knife. Explain that their job is to make a peanut butter and jelly sandwich. There are two rules. First, they are to use only one slice of bread, so the sandwich is really only half a sandwich. The bread may not just be folded over to make the sandwich. The piece of bread must be cut in half to form the two sides of the sandwich. Second, they can use only one hand. The other hand must be kept behind their back at all times. Now have them make the sandwich.

When the sandwiches are completed you are ready for round two. Have everyone get a partner. The partners will now cooperate to make a sandwich. If you

have uneven numbers one person can repeat the activity with a second partner. Give each pair a new piece of bread. The challenge is the same: create a peanut butter and jelly sandwich. Once again, the piece of bread must be cut in half to form the sandwich and each person may only use one hand. Give the teams one minute to plan their strategy before starting. During the strategy planning session, they may not touch the sandwich making materials.

At the completion of the activity, sit back and enjoy a snack of peanut butter and jelly sandwiches.

DISCUSSION IDEAS:

"What" Questions
- Which took longer: when you were working by yourself or with a partner?
- What problems did you have when working by yourself? With a partner?
- What strategies did you use in the second round to the overcome problem of working by yourself?
- How did you feel during the first round? The second round?
- Which sandwich looked better: the first one or the second one?

"So What" Questions
- How did working together affect your efforts?
- What are some tasks where two or more people make the job go easier?
- Are there certain jobs that have to be done by someone working alone? Give examples.
- How does competition affect cooperation?
- Can we be both cooperative and competitive? Explain.
- What happens when people aren't willing to cooperate with each other?

HANDS

- Why would cooperation be important to students at school?
- Why would cooperation be important to people at work?
- Why would cooperation be important to our family?

"Now What" Questions
- How can cooperation help us in our daily lives?
- In what ways can we show cooperation in our family?

Happy Pill

KEY WORDS: Responsibility, Happiness,

LOCATION: In your home

TIME ESTIMATE: 20 minutes plus discussion time

MATERIALS NEEDED:
- 2 clear two liter soda pop bottles for each person.
- About 20 large (slightly hard) marshmallows per person
- Magic markers
- A pair of scissors

Concept

"I'm bored. What can I do?" How many times have you heard this question? Kids think that someone should do something to make them happy. When they talk about being bored or there is nothing to do, they are really asking you to make them happy by finding something to amuse them. Happiness is an emotion that we would like our children to have. It's not that they need to be happy all the time, but at least as a general rule. Too many kids think that happiness comes from other people doing something to make them happy. We need to show them that happiness is a feeling that can be generated from the inside as well as the outside. This activity will allow your family to look at what makes each of us happy and how we can generate that feeling. We must realize that we can do things to make ourselves happy; it is not the responsibility of others to continually make us happy.

Activity

First you will need to have everyone create their "pill" capsule. Give each person 2 two liter soda pop bottles. Remove any labels. Cut the top third off of each bottle. You will now be left with two parts that look somewhat like two halves of a pill capsule. To make one bottle slip into the other bottle, you will need to make a two inch cut in one bottle vertically down the side. This allows the plastic to fold over itself and slip into the other bottle. (If creating the pill itself would be difficult for your children to accomplish, you could do it for them ahead of time.)

Now that you have created your pill capsule, you are ready to make what goes inside. For this step you will use the large marshmallows. It is best if you have let the marshmallows sit out long enough for them to harden up a little. This makes them easier to write on. Using the magic markers, have each person write on the marshmallows things that make them happy. They should write

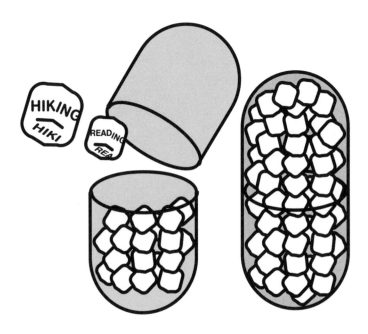

large and put only one "happy thing" on each marshmallow. They should write their "happy thing" on all sides so it can be read from various angles. Now put all of the marshmallows into the two halves and put the halves together. Friction will keep the pill together.

DISCUSSION IDEAS:

"What" Questions
- How hard was it to think up things that make you happy?
- Which items did you write down that cost nothing for you to do?
- Which items cost very little for you to do?
- Which items cost a lot of money for you to do?
- How many things involve doing something with someone else?
- How many things involve doing something by yourself?
- Which things can be done at home?
- Which things involve being somewhere other than home?

"So What" Questions
- How do you act when you are happy?
- How do you act when you are unhappy?
- What are some of the things that make you unhappy?
- Why isn't anyone happy all of the time?
- Are you happier doing things with others or by yourself? Why?
- Do you need money to make you happy? Why or why not?

"Now What" Questions
- What can you do the next time you are feeling unhappy?
- What can you do to help someone who is feeling unhappy?

The idea for this activity was suggested to me by Verne Larsen. Thanks Verne!

He Said . . . She Said

KEY WORDS: Caring, Respect, Gossip, Rumor, Feelings

LOCATION: In your home

TIME ESTIMATE: 10 minutes plus discussion time

MATERIALS NEEDED:
- A trial size (usually less than 1 ounce) tube of toothpaste per participant
- A magic marker
- One piece of paper per person
- One regular table knife per person
- A ruler

Concept

Remember when your parents used to tell you, "If you don't have anything nice to say, don't say anything at all"? What we say has a definite impact on others. Another old saying goes, "Sticks and stones may break my bones but words will never harm me." This saying could not be further from the truth. Words can and do hurt people. Sometimes hurtful things are said out of anger or frustration. Other times they are part of a calculated plan to make someone feel bad. Gossip and rumors affect our children and teens just as much as they affect us. Schools and playgrounds are breeding places for such behavior to take place. The problem is once you say something, how do you take it back? Saying you're sorry doesn't ease the hurt that someone has felt as a result of your words. How do you stop a rumor? Once a rumor has been started, someone is sure to repeat it and even add to the story to make it sound even juicer. The only way to be sure that your words do not harm others is to "think before you speak" (have you ever heard that one before?), because "unsaying" what you have already said is next to impossible.

Activity

Use a magic marker to draw a series of lines vertically on a piece of paper. The lines should be dark and about one quarter of an inch wide and approximately 10 inches long. Make about eight lines on the same piece of paper. You will need one piece of paper with lines for each participant. Give each person a tube of toothpaste. Explain that the object is for each person to see how many of the lines they can cover with toothpaste. The toothpaste must completely cover the line so none of it shows through. Have everyone start together and give them two minutes or until they run out of toothpaste to cover as much of the lines as they can. When time has expired, measure how many inches of the magic marker line each person has covered. The person with the most covered is the winner.

Now pass out a table knife to each person. Explain that they have thirty seconds to see how much of the toothpaste they can fit back into their toothpaste tube. Have them scrape the toothpaste

from the end of one of the covered lines. Once again measure how much of the line they uncovered to see who the winner is.

Discussion Ideas:

"What" Questions
- How many inches did you cover with toothpaste?
- Did you have a hard time getting the toothpaste out of the tube?
- How difficult was it to cover the line?
- Did you roll up the tube or just squeeze it?
- How much toothpaste were you able to get back into the tube?
- Why was it hard to get the toothpaste back into the tube?
- What would you do differently if this activity were repeated?

"So What" Questions
- Can words hurt other people's feelings? Explain.
- If we compare words to toothpaste, how hard is it for us to take back something we said?
- Once harsh or angry words have been spoken, what can we do to help the situation?
- How does anger affect the words we say?
- How do rumors start?
- Why do rumors and gossip spread so fast?
- If you hear a rumor, who is the best person to check with to see if it is true?
- Why would people say, "If you don't have anything nice to say, don't say anything at all"?

"Now What" Questions
- Since we know words can hurt others, what should we do before we speak?
- How can we help stop a rumor once it gets started?
- What should we do if we hurt someone else with our words?

Healthy You

KEY WORDS: Responsibility, Health, Lifestyle, Behavior

LOCATION: Inside your home and a grassy or dirt spot outside onto which you can drop an egg from a height of about ten feet.

TIME ESTIMATE: 30 minutes plus discussion time

MATERIALS NEEDED:
- One raw egg per person
- *The amounts of these materials will be determined by the activity. Please read through the activity to decide how many of each item you think you will need.*
- Masking tape ($\frac{1}{2}$ or $\frac{3}{4}$ of an inch wide)
- Drinking straws
- Napkins
- Facial tissues
- Squares of toilet paper
- Band-Aids
- Cotton balls

Concept

Most people would agree that part of a happy life is being healthy. Certainly there are some illnesses that we can not prevent, but there are behaviors we can practice to promote our own personal health and safety. It is our own responsibility to choose a healthy lifestyle that will allow us the best opportunity to lead a long and healthy life.

Activity

This activity ends with you dropping eggs to the ground from a height of about ten feet. The object is for each person to protect their egg with enough materials that it will not break when hitting the ground. You will determine ahead of time what behaviors will earn the materials that can be used to protect the egg. Each person in your family will answer the questions for themselves. They will then be given the materials as determined by their answers.

Let me give you some examples of how your family can earn these materials. If they get eight hours of sleep on school nights they receive two straws. If they have brushed their teeth everyday for the past seven days they receive three squares of toilet paper. If they wear their seat belt every time they get in a car they receive two cotton balls. If they wear their seat belt most of the time they receive one cotton ball. For each fruit or vegetable they eat on an average day they receive a straw. If they drink a glass of milk each day they receive a tissue. If they do physical activity for at least thirty minutes three times a week they receive three straws. If they wash their hands before meals they receive four squares of toilet paper. For every two glasses of water a day they drink, they receive a straw. If they watch less than two hours of television a day they receive a napkin. If they avoid junk food they receive two Band-Aids. If they take a bath regularly they receive three sheets of toilet paper. You may allow them partial credit. Instead of three straws if they drink three glasses of water a day, you can give them one straw for each glass of water they drink a day. If they wear their seat belt 75% of the time you can give them 75% of a napkin instead of a whole napkin. Everyone receives twenty four inches of masking tape. You can adjust these questions and what they earn to meet the lifestyle of your family. As you consider your questions, make it possible to earn enough materials that there will at least be a chance of not breaking the egg.

You begin the activity by asking everyone the questions that you have decided upon. As your family answers the questions, give them the materials they earn with each answer. When you have asked all of your questions, you should give them their twenty four inches of masking tape. Explain that they have ten minutes to protect their egg using just the materials they have earned from their lifestyle. Tell them that after they have used the materials to protect their egg, you will be dropping the egg to the ground from a height of about ten feet. If you can't find a place to drop the eggs from, you can simply toss them ten feet in the air. If their egg survives without cracking, then they have met the health challenge. If the egg cracks, then they need to consider changing their lifestyle to meet a healthier standard.

DISCUSSION IDEAS:

"What" Questions
- How well did you do earning materials?
- Which questions earned you the most materials? The least materials?
- Which materials were the most helpful in protecting your egg? The least helpful?
- As you were protecting your egg, how confident were you that it would survive the drop?

- Did your egg survive the drop?
- Could your egg have survived if dropped from a greater height?

"So What" Questions
- What can this activity tell us about our lifestyle?
- How often should we practice healthy behavior? Why?
- What are some behaviors, other than the ones for which points were given, that could help us lead a long and healthy life?
- Who is responsible to see that we practice healthy behaviors?
- Should we only practice healthy behaviors while we are still growing? Why or why not?

"Now What" Questions
- What is your reward for practicing healthy behaviors?
- What behavior changes can you make to improve your lifestyle?

I Believe You

KEY WORDS: Honesty, Responsibility, Trust

LOCATION: In the home

TIME ESTIMATE: 15 minutes plus discussion time

MATERIALS NEEDED:
- A deck of playing cards

Concept

The matter of honesty and trust is an important one. Do people believe you? Do people trust you? How do you get people to trust you? How do you lose someone's trust? What happens when you aren't trustworthy? These are all issues that need to be understood by our children and teens. A parent's trust is the very foundation which lets our children and teens assume more responsibility and control over their own lives. The level of trust that they build will determine how much freedom and responsibility they are allowed. Trust is hard to build and easy to destroy. This is true within the context of the family, with friends and in other important areas of life such as school or work.

Activity

Begin by having the dealer deal one card to each player <u>not</u> including themselves. All of the other players, after looking at their card, place their card <u>face down</u> in front of them. The object of the game is for the dealer to guess whether each player's face down card is red or black. To accomplish this, the dealer will ask each player if they have a red or black card face down in front of them. The player may respond truthfully about the card's color or they may lie about the color. The player may describe the card, use body language, tone of voice or other means to convince the dealer to believe their answer. After the player's answer is given, the dealer then states whether they believe the player's answer or not. If they say, "yes, I believe your answer," then both the dealer and the player each receive 5 points. If the dealer accepts the answer that was given by the player, then the player shows their card. It is unimportant whether the player was lying.

But what if the dealer does not believe the answer that the player gave? The player said their card was red, but said it in such a manner that the dealer felt they were lying. At this point the dealer says, "No. I don't believe you." This means that the dealer has challenged the player to prove their answer. Now the player must show their card. If the player was telling the truth and the dealer challenged them, then the player receives 15 points and the dealer loses 5 points. If the player was lying about the color of the card and the dealer challenges them, then the dealer receives 15 points and the player loses 5 points.

This is a contest between the dealer and each player individually. When keeping score, players may end up with negative points. The person with the highest total at the end of the game is the winner. You should play enough rounds that each person gets to be the dealer two or three times. A round is defined as being completed when the dealer has attempted to guess each player's card color. Begin each new round by having new cards dealt by a new dealer.

There are lots of strategies in this game to win points. You may convince the dealer you really are telling the truth and both receive 5 points. You may tell the dealer the right answer but get them to not believe you and challenge you. If you prove them wrong you will get 15 points while the dealer loses 5 points. The dealer may decide a player is lying and challenge them to prove their answer. If they were in fact lying, then the dealer gets 15 points and the player loses 5 points. You decide which strategy will work best for you. Have fun!

DISCUSSION IDEAS:

"What" Questions
- How many points did you get?
- How hard was it to be the dealer?
- How hard was it to choose which person was telling the truth or not?
- How did you decide which people to challenge?
- Which role was more fun, being the dealer or a player? Why?
- Were you usually right or wrong when you made a challenge?
- Did you try to fool the dealer? Why or why not?
- How hard was it to fool the dealer?
- Was your strategy to convince the dealer you were telling the truth so you would both get 5 points? Why or why not?
- How well did your chosen strategy work for you?
- Did you change strategies during the game?

"So What" Questions
- Did you usually tell the truth or try to fool the dealer? Why?
- Were you ever challenged by the dealer? If so, why did he or she single you out to challenge?
- Did you notice any behaviors during the game that would make you trust one of the players less than another? What were these behaviors?

- How do we get people to trust us?
- What events make people lose their trust in us? Give some examples.
- How hard is it to regain someone's trust?
- What do we have to do to regain someone's trust?
- How long does it take to lose someone's trust?
- How long does it take to regain someone's trust?
- Why would we want people to trust us?
- How do the words responsibility and trust go together?
- How does the phrase "making your own decisions" and trust go together?

"Now What" Questions

- Is honesty always rewarded in the short-run? In the long-run?
- How should we behave if we want people to trust us?
- What kinds of behaviors would make others lose their trust in us?
- What does being trustworthy allow us to do that being untrustworthy would not?

I Think I Can

KEY WORDS: Perseverance, Work, Wish, Goal

LOCATION: In your home

TIME ESTIMATE: 10 minutes plus discussion time

MATERIALS NEEDED:
- One ice cube per person with a dime in it

Concept

Not being afraid of hard work and being able to complete a task or job are characteristics that serve us well in today's society. Sometimes we don't always see the results of our hard work until some time in the future. Examples of this could be getting into a good college, a job we enjoy, a dream vacation, etc. These might seem far away when you are in school. But working hard and putting out the effort comes before you reach your goals, not after. Someone once said, "The only place you will find success before work is in the dictionary."

There is a story about a piano player who had just performed a concert. At the end of the concert one of the audience members said to him, "I wish I could play the piano like you can!" He answered, "Do you wish it bad enough that you would be willing to practice eight hours a day for twenty years?" "No," replied the audience member. "Then it will always be just a wish for you," replied the concert pianist. Many people wish for things, but you have to be willing to put in the time and effort to make wishes become reality. You must set your goals and then be willing to work towards them even when the end result may take time to reach.

There are a number of ways to speed up reaching your goal, but not all of these methods are appropriate. If your goal is to be rich, you could rob a bank or sell drugs. However, in the long run, the consequences of how you reach your goal may make the method not worth using. If your goal is to go to a top rated college, but you must cheat on your high school tests to be accepted, you may get into college, but you won't be able to complete the work.

Activity

You will need to prepare a special ice cube for each participant. Freeze a dime inside an ice cube. Try to get the dime as close to the middle of the ice cube as possible. This can be accomplished by filling the ice container half full, freezing it and then putting the dime in. Fill the ice cube container the rest of the way up with water and freeze again.

Once you have prepared the ice cubes, you are ready to begin the activity. Give each person an ice cube after explaining the rules. Explain that the object is to be the first person to get the dime out of the ice cube. The rules are that you may not hit the ice cube with another object nor may you hit the ice cube on anything else such as the table or the floor. You may not put the ice cube in your mouth. You don't want anyone to choke on the ice cube or the coin. You may rub the ice cube with your hands, blow on it or move it back and forth across something to create heat to help you melt the ice cube. The first person to melt their ice cube enough to get the dime out is the winner.

DISCUSSION IDEAS:

"What" Questions
- What methods did you use to melt the ice cube?
- Which of the methods worked the best?
- Did you ever feel like quitting? Why or why not?
- What problems did you encounter?
- If we repeated the activity again, what would you do differently?
- Did you work harder the closer you got to the dime?

"So What" Questions
- How can we compare melting an ice cube to reaching your goals?
- Would you have worked harder if there was more money in the ice cube and only the winner got to keep their money? Why or why not?
- Are some goals worth more work to accomplish than others? Explain.
- Why do the words "work" and "goals" go together?
- Why do some people quit working before reaching their goals?
- Could you have reached the coin quicker by ignoring the rules? Explain.
- Would you feel as successful about reaching your goals if you did so by breaking the rules? Why or why not?

"Now What" Questions
- How does hard work help you reach your goals?
- What are the benefits of reaching your goals through hard work instead of by cheating or taking a short cut?

It All Adds Up

KEY WORDS: Honesty, Shoplifting, Stealing, Cheating

LOCATION: In your home and possibly at a store

TIME ESTIMATE: 30 minutes plus discussion time

MATERIALS NEEDED:
- A piece of paper for each person
- A pen or pencil for each person
- A catalog of office supplies or a trip to the store
- A calculator (this just makes the activity easier)

Concept

Shoplifting is a major problem in our country. Everyone thinks that the store has lots of money and they will never miss one or two little items. But add up the amount that is stolen across the country in a day and you could retire a rich person on it.

The workplace is also full of shoplifters. Of course, they don't think of themselves as shoplifters because it is only small stuff that the huge company they work for will never miss. You know what I'm talking about; bringing home a couple of pens or a box of paper clips from the office, using the office postage meter for personal mail, using the company copier for personal copies, etc. What about stealing time on the job? Examples of this could be making personal phone calls, talking about your weekend on company time, doing personal business, taking an extra ten minutes during lunch or break, etc. There are a lot of little things that are done at the workplace that lower the profit of the business. Each person may only contribute in a small way to this problem, but add up all those small things and you end up with a large bill. Likewise our children should treat classroom supplies like they belong to someone else. Use only what you need and don't waste the school's money.

You can also apply the same concept to cheating at school. If each person only cheats a little, does it add up? How much cheating is really dishonest? Doesn't everyone copy a few answers from their friends? At what point does cheating become dishonest?

Activity

As a group, begin the activity by making a list of office supplies that would be used in a typical office. You might list envelopes, pens, pencils, rulers, scissors, paper clips, file folders, paper, magic markers, etc. Once you have completed this list you need to find out the cost of each item. You can look at the price of a box of paper clips and a package of paper rather than figuring the cost of each individual paper clip or piece of paper. To get these prices you can have the family look through a catalog that has these items or you can all go to a local store that carries these items. Personally I think the store is more fun, but either way works fine.

Once you have the prices, add up the amount it would take to purchase all of them. For example, a pen cost $1.00, a ruler cost $0.90, a pair of scissors cost $1.75, a magic marker $0.89, etc. The total for all of these items would be $4.54. If each worker took these items home during the year or used them on personal business, the amount of money that the business is losing starts to become significant. To see the effect, multiply your total by 100 workers. In the example it would total $454.00

Now let's turn our attention to the time issue. As a group, decide how much an average worker is paid per hour. If you want, you can even choose a specific occupation, like a teacher or retail clerk. Now assume that this worker wastes 15 minutes a day at their job, which is 1 hours per week and 72 hours per year. Multiply the 72 hours by the hourly wage that you have decided upon and you end up with how much money they are stealing from their employer per year. Now multiply that by 100 workers and you can see that we are talking about a large amount of money. Change the time wasted to 30 minutes per day, which is 2 hours per week and 130 hours per year, and see how the total changes.

DISCUSSION IDEAS:

"What" Questions
- Which office supply cost the least? The most?
- Did you expect the office supplies to add up to what they did?
- What was the yearly total wasted by the 100 workers on office supplies?
- Did you expect the hourly costs to add up to what they did?
- What was the yearly total on time wasted by the 100 workers?

"So What" Questions
- Why do people shoplift?
- What are the consequences of getting caught shoplifting?
- Do most people consider taking home a few paper clips stealing? Why or why not?
- Is wasting time on the job really stealing? Why or why not?
- Would the person who owns the business answer these first two questions differently than their employees? Explain.
- How would you answer the first two questions if you were the owner of the business and it was your money they were wasting?

- If you were an employee and you saw someone else taking supplies what would you do?
- If you were an employee and you saw someone not working their full eight hours what would you do?
- Should an employee be fired for taking home a few supplies? Why or why not?
- Should an employee be fired for wasting a half hour a day at work? Why or why not?
- When you waste supplies at school by using more than you need are you stealing? Why or why not?
- How are stealing and cheating related?
- Is cheating on your homework dishonest?
- If you only cheat a little is that O.K.?
- How much cheating is too much?

"Now What" Questions

- How should we treat supplies that someone else has paid for?
- What kind of effort should we put out when we are getting paid to do a job?
- What should we do when asked by a friend to help them by giving them the answer to a homework question?
- What steps can we take to be sure we don't have to cheat at school?

Jack Of All Trades

KEY WORDS: Responsibility, Independence, Self-esteem,
Accomplishment, Self-confidence, Skills

LOCATION: In your home, garage, yard and community

TIME ESTIMATE: This will take place over a period of weeks

MATERIALS NEEDED:
- This will vary according to the skills you decide to teach

Concept

Self-esteem is not something that you can give a person. It's not a warm, fuzzy feeling that comes and goes. Self-esteem is gained one successful experience at a time. Each time you gain a new skill or feel that you can handle a difficult situation, your self-esteem grows. You don't have to wait for huge accomplishments like winning a sporting event or getting on the honor roll to feel this way. Small accomplishments built one on top of another will provide this confidence.

One way for you to assist in the process of self-esteem building is to help your children learn new skills and assume more personal responsibility. The skills that you want to teach them are ones that they will need as they grow older and get ready to take responsibility for their own lives. Sometimes we are too busy or don't even think about passing along everyday skills that will help our children succeed.

Activity

What are the tasks around the house that you accomplish with very little thought? Such things as paying the bills, washing the laundry, putting air in the car tires, fixing a noisy toilet, and changing the furnace filter are all common jobs that need to be done, but how will your children know how to do them unless they are taught? The passing of such knowledge from one generation to another is haphazard in most cases. We do not have a class at school on how to keep your life in order. Our children don't have to have a license that says they know certain skills before they move out of the house. Many of the necessities of life are learned by trial and error. Rather than assuming your children have absorbed how to do all the chores around your house, this activity asks you to set up a formal process by which this is done. Look around your house and decide what you would want your children to be able to do when they move out.

Start by listing all of the things that are done at your house. These might include sorting the laundry, operating the washer and dryer, loading the dishwasher, mopping the kitchen floor, checking and adding oil to the car, checking the windshield washer fluid on the car, changing a flat tire, the different functions for a number of common tools, fixing the toilet when it begins to make noise, understanding the electrical fuse box to your house, finding out how to shut off the water to your house in an emergency, knowing where to find emergency numbers in the phone book, sewing a button on a shirt, shopping for bargains, using coupons at the grocery store, reading the ingredients label, cooking a couple of basic meals, addressing an envelope, writing a check, balancing a check book, setting up a budget, what interest payments are, how do credit cards work, etc. I could continue, but I think you get the idea.

Once you have decided the tasks you would like to teach, divide them into categories such as kitchen, shopping, finance, cars, household repairs, yard work, etc. Then assign each of your tasks to one of these categories. These categories are going to become skill badges similar to the merit badges in the Boy Scouts or Girl Scouts. Create a master list of the categories and the skills that need to be learned under each category. This list becomes a checklist for your children. To complete the learning of a task they must master it to your satisfaction. You will be the final judge.

If you have a wide spread of ages in your family, then make lists that match each child's abilities. For each category decide what the proper recognition should be for learning all of the skills in that category. Give them some kind of homemade certificate, take them out for ice cream, buy them something that they have been wanting, etc., when they complete a category. You may want to reward them with something small for each category and then a larger reward when the entire list has been finished. Give them a deadline to accomplish their list.

It is now time to call the family together. Explain the activity. Go through the list of skills to be learned. Go over the reward system that can be earned. Point out the deadline. Meet once a week to see how they are doing on their lists. If you feel weak in an area that you want them to learn, find someone who can teach them those particular skills. You can learn right along with them. You can repeat this activity again the next year or so when they are ready to learn a new set of skills.

DISCUSSION IDEAS:

"What" Questions
- Which tasks were easy for you to learn? More difficult?
- Which tasks were the most fun to learn? Least fun?
- Which tasks did you find the most interesting? Least interesting?
- Which tasks do you think will be most useful to you when you move out of the house? Least useful?

"So What" Questions
- How confident do you feel about the tasks that you learned?
- Could you do them now by yourself?
- Could you teach these tasks to someone else?
- How does it make you feel when you know you can accomplish something that you couldn't do before?
- What would you like to learn how to do in the future?
- Does knowing how to complete these tasks make you a better person? Why or why not?
- Does knowing how to complete these tasks give you more self-confidence? Why or why not?

"Now What" Questions
- How does knowing how to do different tasks make you more independent?
- Why is it important to be independent?

Jobs, Jobs and More Jobs

KEY WORDS: Responsibility, Career, Occupation, Job, Status

LOCATION: In the community

TIME ESTIMATE: Several days over a period of weeks or even months

MATERIALS NEEDED:
- A spiral notebook per child
- A pen or pencil per child

Concept

How many times do our children get asked, "What do you want to be when you grow up?" The choice of a career is so important to our children's future happiness that we need to take an active role in that choice. Most school districts today are starting to ask about career choices by the ninth grade. There are a number of federal and state funded programs that help our kids choose a career. If you ask most kids what they want to be, their choices center around certain well known occupations. You will hear such jobs as lawyer, doctor, teacher, engineer, nurse, police officer, secretary, etc. Even though these might be the most common answers, they make up only a small percentage of jobs in the work force.

There are literally hundreds of different job classifications listed by the government. We need to make our children aware of the broad array of job possibilities to choose from. How can they make an informed decision unless they have a chance to see what the various fields look like? As an added benefit, when your kids become interested in a certain career, their interest in school goes up because they now have a reason to get good grades. Even if they change their mind ten times before settling on the career that is right for them, you have helped to motivate them. It is the responsibility of each person to prepare themselves to make a living. Choosing the right career will help in meeting that responsibility.

Activity

This activity is easy to describe, but time consuming to do. It is basically a call for you to tour a number of work places that do the kind of work your children might be interested in. Don't make the mistake of limiting your visits to places your children would like to visit. What you want to do is to open their eyes up to a lot of different kinds of opportunities. Before choosing a career, you should know a lot about it. This can only be done by experiencing the sights and sounds of the work place.

Look around your town and make a list of the places you would like to visit. If you know someone there, that's all the better but you don't have to. You can call any work place and ask to speak to someone in charge. Explain to them that you are trying to expose your children to a number of different types of occupations and you would like to take a tour of their business. Most businesses will be willing to accommodate you. If the business is only open during the school week, visit late in the day, during a school vacation or during the summer. If you can't take any time off of your own job, make all of the arrangements and find a responsible teen or other adult to take your kids. Use part of your vacation time to visit places that are not local. Call ahead and set up a tour. Our family spent many a day while on vacation touring lumber mills, factories, colleges, military facilities, law related fields, etc. It was worth every hour.

Don't just visit. You want to get the most out of each trip. Give each child a "career" notebook. They can use the notebook to keep a record of each visit. Before you go have them write down a list of questions they would like answered during the visit. The questions may be about working conditions, salary levels, education needed to get hired, what they produce or how they sell their product. This way during the visit, your kids will know what to talk about. Have them record the answers to their questions in their notebook. After the visit have them write about their impressions of the tour. They can indicate if they saw anybody doing something that looked like something they would like to do. They may write that they definitely don't want to go into that field and tell why. They may have additional questions that they would like answered. The notebook will document their visit and their feelings about that work place as a career possibility.

DISCUSSION IDEAS:

"What" Questions (To be asked after each tour)

- What were the questions that you wanted answered before you went? Did they get answered?
- What were your impressions?
- What was the most interesting part of the tour? The least interesting?
- What looked like the easiest job at the work place? The hardest?
- Which jobs looked like the highest paying jobs? The lowest paying?
- Which jobs looked like the most fun? The most boring?
- What one word or phrase would you choose to describe the business?

"So What" Questions (To be asked after you visit a number of places)

- How do you think the job you choose affects your life?
- What does education have to do with the career you choose?
- Does the amount of money you earn determine if you like your job? Why or why not?
- Why is it important for people to work in our society?
- Are some jobs considered to be more important than others? Explain.
- Does the job you have affect your status in the community? Explain.

"Now What" Questions

- While you are still in school, how can you best prepare for a career that you will enjoy?
- How does your choice of a career affect the rest of your life?

Knowledge Not Magic

KEY WORDS: Responsibility, Knowledge, Education, Decision Making

LOCATION: In your home

TIME ESTIMATE: 15 minutes plus discussion time

MATERIALS NEEDED:
- 15 pennies

Concept

The more information you have concerning a situation, the better decision you can make. If you already know the answer to a problem, you are way ahead of someone who is just starting to find out the answer. This can be true in the field of alcohol, tobacco and other drugs as well as such areas as sexually transmitted diseases. You don't have to experience the problems associated with these issues if you already know the consequences connected with them. Knowledge is power! We can't guarantee that our children will succeed just because of what they know, but is does give them an advantage over others.

This is not only true in making decisions, but also in areas such as free time, social life, school, sports or games. When you know what is expected of you and follow the guidelines that have been set up, you have a much better chance of succeeding. If the household rule is "do your homework before you do anything else after school," then do it and everything else will go much smoother. With responsibility comes the freedom to make your own decisions. But with that freedom also comes the responsibility to make appropriate decisions.

Activity

Place fifteen pennies on a table or the floor. Have someone else be the challenger to play this game with you. The game goes like this. You each take turns taking one, two or three of the pennies during each turn. The loser is the person who has to pick up the last penny. The key for you as the expert is to remember that you want to try to get pennies number two, six and ten. If you are able to pick these pennies up, especially number ten, then you will always be the winner. Be sure to keep track of what your challenger takes. You need to add what you take and what they take together when trying to get pennies number two, six and ten. It is the total number of pennies that have been taken that is important, not just how many you yourself have taken. It doesn't matter who goes first in this game. Give your challenger the option of going first or second to be sure that they have every opportunity to beat you.

Here is an example. The challenger takes one penny on their first pick. You would then take only one penny since you are trying to be the one that takes penny number two. The challenger now takes three pennies. A total of five pennies have now been taken. Since you want to pick up penny number six you would take one penny. Let's say that the challenger next takes two pennies for a total of eight pennies. You would take two pennies because you are trying to get the tenth penny.

Once you have the tenth penny, there is no way for the challenger to beat you. No matter what combination they use, they will lose by having to pick up the last penny. Give others an opportunity to challenge you. They can even get advice from the rest of the group. You may get beat once in a while by someone who lucks out and picks up the correct number of pennies. If that happens simply challenge them again. For unless they know why they beat you, the chances are they won't be able to do it again. After a few rounds if they haven't been able to guess the winning strategy, explain what the secret to the game is.

DISCUSSION IDEAS:

"What" Questions
- How hard was it to beat the expert?
- Why was it hard to beat the expert?
- What did the expert know that you didn't know?
- How easy would it be for you to be the expert now that you know the secrets?

"So What" Questions
- How much of an advantage is it in a game to know something that the rest of the players don't know?
- Name some other examples where information can be an important factor in how well you do something.
- How much power does information give you?
- How can we relate information to staying away from such things as alcohol, tobacco, drugs or sexual behavior?
- Who can you gather information from that will help you keep your body healthy?
- Are there times when you get information that is incorrect? What happens then?
- How can the wrong information hurt you?
- Explain this phrase: "Knowledge is power."

"Now What" Questions
- How does knowledge or information give you an advantage over others?
- How can we use knowledge or information to help us make a decision?

Maid Service

Concept

One day I was driving down the street and watched a young man toss his soft drink cup on the ground. I don't know who he thought was going to clean up after him, but he didn't seem too worried about it. Maybe he came from a house where they had a maid who followed him around and cleaned up after him. Well, in the real world people should be responsible for themselves. I didn't get a chance to ask him why he did this. However, from other conversations I have had with youth, I probably would have gotten an answer something like "People are paid to pick up trash. I am just helping them keep their job."

Our society spends entirely too much tax money hiring people to clean up roadways, parks, recreation areas, and other places frequented by people who should know better than to throw their trash on the ground. We even had to start a national volunteer highway cleanup campaign where people and organizations adopt a stretch of highway and are responsible to clean up other people's trash to keep the highways looking nice. This is absurd! If everyone took care of their own trash, then others wouldn't have to clean up after them. This is called responsibility. If people didn't have to volunteer their time cleaning up other people's trash, then their time could be devoted to more worthwhile community projects.

Activity

Gather up the family and announce that you are going to help out the community today. Take them to an area of town that needs some cleaning up. This could be a recreation area, retail location or highway. If you choose a highway, be sure that your children understand the danger involved from passing cars. Set a goal for your family. You can work a set amount of time, collect a certain amount of trash or clean a certain area or length of roadway. To make the work more light-hearted, work in pairs or in a group. This will allow for interaction and conversation to take place during the activity. One way to increase the satisfaction of a job well done is to take a before and after picture of the area. Have your family posed in both pictures to help make the connection between a need in the community and filling that need through community service. When you get the picture developed, hang it on the refrigerator or some other prominent place as a reminder to your family. This is an activity that can be repeated once a year.

Why did I choose cleaning up litter as opposed to helping out at a nursing home or cleaning up a senior citizen's yard? Because I wanted to have your children understand the uselessness of litter. The bottom line is that when someone thoughtlessly throws litter on the ground, someone else has to clean it up. There are any number of community service projects that can be undertaken, but they don't convey the utter uselessness of cleaning up trash that shouldn't have been there in the first place. How can the litter problem be stopped? By everyone taking responsibility for their own actions.

DISCUSSION IDEAS:

"What" Questions
- How would you describe the area before we started cleaning it up?
- How would you describe it now?
- How much trash did we collect?
- What was the most common kinds of things we found?
- What was the most unique thing we found?
- What was the yuckiest thing we found?
- How hard is it to pick up trash?
- How long do you think it has been since this place has been cleaned up?
- How many people must have littered to make this much of a mess?
- Explain how picking up litter provides a service to the community.
- Did any of this litter come about "naturally," or could it all have been avoided if people were more responsible? Explain.

"So What" Questions
- How did you feel about picking up after someone else?
- Do you think that now that we have made the place clean people will stop littering? Why or why not?
- What other things would you rather have been doing today instead of picking up trash?
- What can this experience teach us about people?
- Why is it important for each person to clean up after themselves?
- Who pays for the people who are hired to clean up litter?

"Now What" Questions
- What can we do to help the litter problem?
- How is littering a matter of responsibility?
- What can we do at home to exhibit responsibility?

Map Master

KEY WORDS: Perseverance, Planning, Goal,

LOCATION: In your home

TIME ESTIMATE: 30 minutes plus discussion time

MATERIALS NEEDED:
- A map for each team of two
- A pen or pencil for each team
- A piece of paper for each team

Concept

When we think of perseverance we think of hard work and not giving up. However, that is not all there is to persevering. To overcome an obstacle, meet a deadline or succeed when things look tough, we need more than just hard work. The ability to think ahead and to plan a course of action involving a series of steps to reach a goal is critical to success. Each of us needs to be able to visualize what steps need to be taken to get from point A to point B when working on a project or towards a goal. What are the obstacles that must be overcome? What are the tools we will need to accomplish the job? In what order should we complete each step? How much time will be needed? What are the priorities? Being able to plan will get you a long way toward being able to succeed.

Activity

Divide your family into teams of two. If you have an uneven number, one person can complete the activity by themselves. Give each team a map that covers at least three hundred miles from one edge of the map to the other. You may provide these maps in a couple of ways. You can give each team a different map or you can get copies of the same map for each team. Your local Chamber of Commerce or nearest Tourist Information Center will probably have maps you can get for free.

Explain that each team is going to take a trip together. Each team picks their own starting and ending place on the map. The starting and ending points must be at least three hundred miles apart. They will be leaving on Friday morning and must be home by Monday night. Give each team about twenty minutes to write down the answers to the following questions.

1. How many miles is it from the starting point to the ending point if you take the most direct route?
2. As you drive to your destination, in which direction will you be traveling most of the time? (North, South, East or West)
3. If you average fifty miles an hour as you travel, how long will it take you to reach your destination if you do not have to stop?
4. If you average twenty miles to the gallon as you travel, how many gallons of gas will you use to get there?
5. Where will you stop to have a meal?
6. Will you take other breaks besides the stop for a meal? What would these stops be for?
7. What items will you need to have with you in the car to make the trip safe and enjoyable?
8. What are some of the points of interest along the way that you would like to visit?
9. How many miles is it from the starting point to the ending point if you leave the most direct route and make side trips to these points of interest?
10. What are some of the activities you could do while at your destination?

11. What will you need to pack to stay at your destination?
12. How much money will you need for this trip?
13. What are some of the things that could happen to you on this trip to ruin it?

When everyone has finished answering the questions, have each team state their starting and ending points and then read their answers aloud.

DISCUSSION IDEAS:

"What" Questions
- How hard was it to answer the questions?
- What was the easiest question to answer? The hardest?
- Was it easy to come to an agreement between the partners?
- What part did math play in determining your answers?
- How would the answers to some of the questions change depending on where in the country you were traveling?

"So What" Questions
- Why is planning important when you are taking a trip?
- Who could you have asked for help in planning your trip?
- How do you have to use planning at school?
- In what other areas of your life is planning important?
- How does planning help us reach our goals and complete projects?
- How does having a plan help us to make better decisions?
- What do you do if after you have made your plans things change?

"Now What" Questions
- How does planning help us to succeed?
- Where can you find help when making a plan?

Marble Slide

KEY WORDS: Cooperation, Perseverance, Problem Solving, Teamwork, Brainstorming

LOCATION: In your home

TIME ESTIMATE: 30 minutes plus discussion time

MATERIALS NEEDED:
- You need to start collecting for this activity early. It requires a lot of cardboard tubes. These tubes come from paper towel rolls, toilet paper rolls, gift wrapping paper rolls, etc. Ask your friends to help you collect these.
- About 10 feet of cardboard tubes for each team
- A roll of masking tape (1/2 inch wide would be fine) for each team
- A pair of scissors for each team
- A chair for each team
- A marble for each team
- A watch with a second hand

Concept

Today's world requires us to be able to solve problems that require critical thinking. All problems do not have only one right answer nor is the answer to some problems easily recognizable. Rather than teaching the "right" answer to a problem, this activity shows that sometimes there is more than one way to solve a problem. The activity encourages the participants to think in creative ways to reach their goal. Since the activity is done with a partner or in teams, it also gives the participants a chance to work together and experience the problems and rewards of being part of a team.

Activity

Divide into teams of two or three people. If there are only two people participating in this activity, have each of them work alone. Explain that this activity involves a competition between the teams. Each team will get a marble, a chair, some masking tape, scissors and an equal length of cardboard tubes. The object is to use these items to make a cardboard run for the marble to roll down. They will have 12 minutes to construct their slide. The winning team will be the one that makes the marble stay in the tubes the longest without allowing the marble to stop. So speed is not the object, time is the object. The teams can use the chair to attach the cardboard to. This will allow the height they need to get the marble rolling. They may not use any other objects to help them. They may only allow the cardboard to touch the floor at the end of the slide. Allow them to use as much masking tape as they need to connect their tubes.

Do not give them too many instructions. You want them to solve this problem on their own. Have the teams construct their slides in different areas, if possible, so they can't pick up any ideas from the other team. At the end of their building time, have a competition to see which team's slide made the marble travel through it for the longest time. Let all the participants watch the timing of each slide.

Now have them repeat the activity. Have the teams cut the tubes apart so they can be reused. If none of the teams thought to cut the cardboard tubes in half the long way using their scissors, you can mention this before starting again. This will allow the slide to be twice as long. Ask them if they thought about making turns, hills, etc. Require that the teams brainstorm ideas among themselves for about two minutes without touching the tubes before starting the second round. This will force them to think of different ways to solve the problem rather than just start building. Once again give them 12 minutes to complete the slide and then repeat the time test again.

DISCUSSION IDEAS:

"What" Questions
- How did you decide what your slide would look like in the first round? In the second round?
- Did everyone on the team give equal input on how to design the slide? Why or why not?
- What were the problems you encountered in the first round?
- Did you start building right away or did you spend some time planning first?
- How well did your design work?
- Did your team run out of time before finishing?
- What changes did you make in the second round?
- Did you copy any ideas from other teams in the second round?
- Did your time improve in the second round? Why or why not?
- What would you do differently if you had a third round?

"So What" Questions

- Did only one person on your team have all of the answers to the problem?
- Did you hear any good ideas from others that you had not thought of yourself?
- What did each person add to the team?
- How well did your team work together?
- How can working together allow us to better solve problems?
- Is it easier to solve problems by yourself or with the help of others? Explain.
- Is it O.K. to copy another team's ideas? Why or why not?
- How can brainstorming help us find solutions to a problem?

"Now What" Questions

- How can others help us solve a problem?
- When is working together as a team to solve a problem better than working by ourselves?
- Should we always take the first answer we think of to solve a problem? Why or why not?

Mealtime R Us

KEY WORDS: Caring, Self-esteem, Talents, Unique, Special, Characteristics

LOCATION: In your home

TIME ESTIMATE: 30 minutes plus discussion time

MATERIALS NEEDED:
- One 18 inch by 24 inch piece of posterboard for each person
- A variety of magic markers, colored pencils, crayons
- Scissors
- Magazines and newspapers that show pictures of activities or interests that your kids have
- Glue
- Any personal items that your children have that show their interests
- Clear contact paper or access to a laminating machine

Concept

There are unique characteristics that make up each one of us. It is these characteristics that make each one of us special. Many kids have not even considered what unique talents they have or how special they are. Taking time to sit down and reflect on what makes them who they are is an experience that can bring long-lasting results. This activity allows you to combine talking about what makes your children unique with the magic of repetition. Advertising has proven that the more times you hear and see something, the greater the likelihood that you will remember it. Repetition allows us to internalize thoughts and realizations that will help build our self-esteem. The place mats will also allow the entire family to become aware of each others special characteristics.

Activity

This activity involves making a place mat that can be used at mealtime. Give each person a piece of posterboard. Explain that on one side of the place mat each person will create a collage of pictures, drawings, sayings, and any other items that would represent things they like. This side of the place mat answers the question "What I like is . . ." Some examples of this would be cats, stuffed animals, baseball, rap music, pizza, playing the piano, my friends, talking on the phone, summer, going to Disneyland, etc.

The other side of the place mat will answer the question of "What makes me who I am is . . ." Once again, this should be represented with a collage of pictures, drawings, sayings, and any other items that would represent things that tell who they are. Some examples of this would be funny, happy, thoughtful, caring, helpful, smart, good at music, a good listener, people like me, have lots of friends, a good brother/sister, keep a clean room, etc. This side is harder than the "things I like side," which is why we do it second. You may have to help younger children understand this concept by discussing a few examples either about yourself or about them. Do not get carried away giving them help, part of the activity is for them to spend some time thinking about the characteristics that together make them who they are.

How each person decides to represent each side of the place mat should be left up to them. They can have mainly pictures cut out of a magazine, pictures they draw themselves, words, phrases, decals, ticket stubs from events they have attended, newspaper articles about sports or people they like, etc. They can add doodles or designs to help them complete the overall look. Be sure that their name is on the place mat somewhere along with the date it was created.

When both sides of the place mat have been completed, you can use clear contact paper to cover it to make it resist liquids and be washable. If you want a sturdier finish, you can find a laminating machine. Many times one is available at your local school, public library or copy shop. The cost for this service is usually minimal.

Once the place mats have been created, you should use them at least once a week during a meal. This allows the repetition that is needed to help remind our kids of who they are and why they are unique. This is an activity that can be repeated every year. If you keep the place mats from previous years, you will end up with a pretty good record of your child over the years. When your children grow up and start families of their own, these could be a great housewarming gift. They could also be saved and used when your kids come back to visit. They make great conversation starters about "the good old days." Wouldn't the grandchildren love to see what their mom or dad were like when they were their age?

DISCUSSION IDEAS:

"What" Questions
- How many different types of art did you use to create your place mat?
- How hard was it to think of things that you like?
- How hard was it to think of characteristics about you?
- Which side has more items on it: the things you like or characteristics about you?

- How balanced are your likes? Are there many different things or lots of items about one thing?
- Did you discover anything about yourself as you chose what to put on each side?

"So What" Questions

- How do the things we like make us different than other people?
- How do our characteristics make us unique?
- Should we try to be like someone else? Why or why not?
- What makes it hard to be like someone else?
- What would happen if everyone liked the same things?
- What unique things does each person bring to our family?
- What would happen if everyone had the same characteristics?
- How are you different from others in your family?
- How are you the same as others in your family?

"Now What" Questions

- Why is it good for each person to be special and unique?
- How does knowing more about each other help to strengthen the family?

Memories

> **KEY WORDS:** Caring, Responsibility, Bonding, Memories, Goals, Support
>
> **LOCATION:** In and around your home
>
> **TIME ESTIMATE:** 30 minutes and one year plus discussion time
>
> **MATERIALS NEEDED:**
> - 6 to 10 half sheets of notebook paper for each person
> - A pen or pencil for each person
> - A large container (such as a jar or box) that can be buried or hidden

Concept

Memories bind families together. It is the everyday activities and special events that occur throughout the year that makes each family unique. In our busy and fast paced world, we can forget the events and stories that make up our family history. Our likes, dislikes, special events, humorous stories, and momentous occasions need to be recorded each year so we can bring them back to life. As your family talks about the past and relives the exciting times, the feelings that are shared help to cement relationships and bond the family together. A yearly review of these memories is a great tradition to start in your family. This activity can give you a chance to discuss how the things we do together as a family and the memories that we share give us a common foundation which can help to enhance the good times and get us through the tough times.

Another aspect of this activity is a review of both family and personal goals. Your family should have goals they are trying to reach both as a group and as individuals. By sharing these goals, everyone has a chance to support each other to accomplish both the family and the individual goals. However, even though others can support us as we try to reach our goals, it is still our own responsibility to work towards accomplishing our goals.

Activity

Your family is going to create a time capsule. It will be kept hidden for one year from the date that you seal it. The time capsule will have a number of things placed in it. Each list, memory or goal that is placed in the time capsule should identify who created it. If it is a family list, then just identify it with the word "family." Here are some suggestions of what should go in the time capsule: A list of family goals that you would like to accomplish as a family during the next year. A list of individual goals that each person would like to accomplish during the next year. A newspaper dated on or near the date that you seal the time capsule. A photocopy of some of the accomplishments that the members of your family earned over the last year. An item (or a description of the item) from each person that they can give up for a year that tells something about themselves. An individual list telling what makes them happy. An individual list of what each person likes to do for fun. A list of the friends you hang out with. A list of favorite family meals. Each person could write down a couple of memories from the past year that were really special, funny or exciting. You could even put in some photos that you can give up for a year. The idea is to have in the time capsule a representation of the things that you did over the last year and a list of the goals you would like to accomplish during the next year.

Now it is time for the burial ceremony. You should surround this with a lot of ritual. Have a special dinner, use candles, read an uplifting poem, go through and read all of the material in the time capsule, bury the capsule or put it away in a safe place and close with a group hug. Seal the container so moisture or animals won't bother it. Be sure to mark the area well so you can find it again. Then in one year have another ceremony where you dig it up and go through the contents as a family. It should be a great time to once again share your memories, to see if you still like the same things and to talk about the family and individual goals.

DISCUSSION IDEAS:
(Have your discussion right after you bury the capsule.)

"What" Questions
- How easy was it to remember what happened in our family during the last year?
- What kinds of events do we end up remembering?
- Which list was the easiest to come up with? Why?
- Which list was the hardest to come up with? Why?
- What were the individual goals that you wrote down?
- How hard was it to come up with family goals? Why?
- What special meaning did the item you contributed have to you?

"So What" Questions
- How does this capsule represent you as a person?
- How does this capsule represent us as a family?
- In what ways do you think we will change over the next year?
- How can we be sure that we reach our family goals?
- How can we help each other reach our individual goals?
- How can memories help bond our family together?
- How does knowing more about each other allow us to be a better family?

"Now What" Questions

• What can each of us do to help strengthen our family over the next year?

• What steps will you need to take to reach your goals in a year?

• What specific actions can we take to help each other reach our family and individual goals?

Mother Teresa

KEY WORDS: Caring, Forgiveness, Grudge, Quality of Life

LOCATION: In your home

TIME ESTIMATE: 10 minutes plus discussion time

MATERIALS NEEDED:
- Two large drinking glasses
- Food coloring
- Bleach, such as Clorox

Concept

Have you ever heard the phrase, "I don't get mad, I get even!"? It may sound humorous, but in reality it can be quite damaging to our peace of mind. Holding a grudge against someone can gnaw at our insides and cause us to become bitter and unhappy. When someone has done something to us, the best course of action is to explain to them why you feel the way you do and to "forgive and forget." Otherwise you will be carrying the pain with you, and eventually that bitterness will start to affect other areas of your life. Carrying a grudge doesn't increase your quality of life, and in many cases can actually diminish it. Forgiving someone for something doesn't always mean that you can forget about it right away, but it does mean that you can begin moving on. As you go through the process of forgiving you reduce the pain. Holding onto that feeling will only increase your pain over time.

Activity

This activity is a demonstration. Be careful with smaller children when using the bleach. Fill one of the large drinking glasses about a quarter full with water. Fill the other large drinking glass a little more than half full with bleach. Gather the family around the glasses in a position where everyone can clearly see. Put one drop of food coloring into the glass of water. Do not stir the water. Allow the drop of food coloring to drift throughout the water.

After about a minute, the food coloring will have spread throughout the glass. At this point you can swirl the water a couple of times to completely distribute the food coloring throughout the water. Take a moment to observe how the food coloring has completely changed the color of the water. Put one drop of bleach into the glass of colored water. Watch the reaction. Now pour the entire half glass of bleach into the glass of colored water. After about a minute, you can give the glass a swirl to completely mix the bleach with the water. As you watch the water, it will begin to change back to a clear color.

DISCUSSION IDEAS:

"What" Questions

- How long did it take for the food coloring to completely color the water?
- Did one drop of bleach have any impact on the food coloring?
- How much bleach did we have to use to clear up the water?
- Did the bleach clear up the water immediately? How long did it take?

"So What" Questions
- How can we compare the drop of food coloring with someone making us feel bad?
- How can holding a grudge against someone make us unhappy?
- How can a grudge affect our outlook on life?
- Why is it better to "forgive and forget" than hold a grudge?
- How can forgiving help us in our relationships with others?

"Now What" Questions
- How does forgiving make our lives better?

Mr. Rogers

KEY WORDS: Caring, Service to Others, Community Service

LOCATION: In your home

TIME ESTIMATE: 20 minutes plus discussion time

MATERIALS NEEDED:
- Cassette tape recorder
- Blank cassette tape
- 1 children's storybook per person

Concept

Doing something for others without expecting anything in return is one value that helps to keep our society functioning. Community service not only enhances the community at large, but has a positive impact on individuals as well. It can help us realize that there are others who are less fortunate than we are and that we have it in our power to help them. It isn't always money that solves problems. Sometimes it just takes someone who is willing to take some of their free time and spend it helping others.

Activity

This activity involves recording a child's story on cassette tape. Buy an inexpensive child's story book. If cost is an issue, these can be picked up used at garage sales, thrift stores and from families whose children are outgrowing their books. Each person will read a story into the tape recorder. Have the reader use a variety of different voices to represent each of the characters in the story. Another possibility would be to have different people read the parts of the characters in the story. Be sure that everyone practices before you do the final recording. Have them read slowly and with plenty of expression. Be sure to pause at the end of each page to allow the listening reader a chance to turn the page when they are following along. Since the children who could be listening to this story might not be able to follow along as you read, you will have to tell them when to turn each page. After recording the story, go back and listen to it while following along to make sure everything is O.K.

Once you have completed the recording there are lots of things you can do with it. You can donate the book and the cassette tape to a library, hospital, preschool, another family, church nursery, etc.

If you are going to give the cassette tape to a child that you know, then you can make it really special by personalizing the tape. At certain points in the story you can stop, call the child by name and ask them a question about the story. Pause long enough for them to answer and then go on. At the end of the story you can tell them how much fun it was to share this story with them.

DISCUSSION IDEAS:

"What" Questions
- How hard was it to choose a good story?
- How did you know what kinds of voices to use for the characters?
- Did it feel funny to read with different voices?
- How do you think you sounded on tape?

- If you were to record the story over again, what would you do differently?

"So What" Questions

- How do you think a child will react when they listen to this cassette?
- Would you like to see them listen to it? Why or why not?
- How can helping others make us feel good?
- How can helping others make our community a better place to live?
- What are some ways that people are helping others in our community?

"Now What" Questions

- What can we do to help individuals in our community?
- What can we do to help our community be a better place to live?

My Country – My Family

KEY WORDS: Respect, Beliefs, Belonging, Unite, Patriotism, Loyalty

LOCATION: In your home

TIME ESTIMATE: 30 minutes plus discussion time

MATERIALS NEEDED:
- A dictionary
- Two pieces of paper for each person
- A pen or pencil for each person
- A set of crayons, markers or colored pencils

Concept

Feeling like we belong is a need that we all have. But we don't want to just belong to anything, we want to belong to something that is bigger than we are. This need to belong can be satisfied through the family. If it is not satisfied through the family, then our children will look elsewhere. This feeling of belonging is a major factor in gang membership. Once this feeling of belonging is found, there develops a fierce loyalty to the group that binds the members together.

Patriotism is built on this feeling of belonging. We are all members of a certain country and when other members of our country are threatened, then we all feel threatened. We respond with a feeling of anger. When our country defends itself, there is a uniting together against the attacking group that is trying to destroy what we believe in. Or in another context, during the Olympics our citizens unite behind our athletes to cheer them on to victory against competing countries.

I believe that respect for our country begins with respect for our family. When something happens to one of our family members, the entire family needs to pull together and support one another. This feeling of belonging comes from respecting what a family, group or organization stands for and being willing to stand up for those beliefs and values.

Activity

Give each person a piece of paper and a pen or pencil. Have everyone write out the Pledge of Allegiance on their paper. See if they can write it from memory, then check to see how well they did. The pledge reads, "I pledge allegiance to the flag of the United States of America and to the Republic for which it stands, one nation under God, indivisible, with liberty and justice for all." Now go through the pledge and define certain words. Be sure that everyone understands the following: pledge, allegiance, flag, United States of America, Republic, which it stands, nation, your understanding of God, indivisible, liberty and justice for all. You can use dictionary definitions to begin with, but be sure that you discuss what these words mean using everyday language and by using examples from everyday life.

Now pass out a blank piece of paper to each person and make the crayons, markers or colored pencils available. Have each person create a flag that has pictures of things that represent themselves and your family. Have them include drawings that would show things that they and the family like to do, as well as things that they and the family believe in and value. When completed, have everyone describe what they have drawn and share how those items represent themselves and the family.

As a concluding activity have the family as a group rewrite the Pledge of Allegiance as a family pledge. Substitute words that reflect a personalized pledge of the things that your family believes are important and values. Display the flags and the family pledge in a prominent place for a week.

DISCUSSION IDEAS:

"What" Questions

- Were you able to correctly write the Pledge of Allegiance from memory?
- How well could you define the words found in the Pledge of Allegiance?
- Did you have a hard time coming up with things to draw on your flag about yourself? Your family?
- What was one interesting thing that someone else drew?
- What did someone else draw that surprised you?
- Did anyone else draw something similar to what you drew?
- How hard was it to write the family pledge?

"So What" Questions

- Why is respect for your country important?
- How do we show respect for our country?
- Why is respect for our family important?
- What does it feel like to belong to a group?
- How do people decide which groups to belong to?
- How is belonging to a family different than belonging to another group?
- What do the words in the Pledge of Allegiance tell us about our country?
- What do the words we used in our family pledge tell us about our family?

"Now What" Questions

- How can we show respect for our family and the people in our family?
- How can we create a feeling of belonging in our family?

Mystery Drug

KEY WORDS: Responsibility, Illegal Drugs, Choice, Decision, Consequences, Peer Pressure

LOCATION: In your home

TIME ESTIMATE: 8 minutes plus discussion time

MATERIALS NEEDED:
- 5 water glasses
- 1 tablespoon
- 3 tablespoons of talcum powder
- 3 tablespoons of baking soda
- 3 tablespoons of flour
- 3 tablespoons of powdered confectioners sugar
- 1 cup of vinegar

Concept

Illegal drugs don't come with a guarantee. When you put a drug into your body, there are so many variables that you really don't know what the reaction of your body will be. You may have a weak heart or some other internal defect that you don't even know about. Then there is the uncertainty of the drugs themselves. Since street drugs are not made to conform with any federal laws, you don't know what goes into them. There have been numerous reports of rat poison, talcum powder and other chemicals that have been used to make a drug stretch farther in order to allow the drug dealers to make a larger profit.

What you see is not always what you get, and there are no "truth in advertising" laws for the drug dealers to worry about. The best way to deal with the problem of what is really in a drug you have been offered is to say, "No Thanks." It is your choice as to whether you use drugs or not. Once you make the choice, you are responsible for whatever consequences might occur from making that decision.

Activity

Before bringing the family together for the activity, put 3 tablespoons of each powder into 4 separate glasses. One type of powder goes in each glass. Crush the powders up so they look as much alike as possible. Pour approximately eight ounces of vinegar into the fifth glass. You don't want anyone to see you do this or the mystery will be solved before you even begin.

Begin the activity by showing all four powders to your children and ask them to decide which one will cause a chemical reaction when mixed with a liquid. Do not tell them what the liquid or powders are or in any way identify them. Have each person indicate which powder they think looks the most likely to cause a chemical

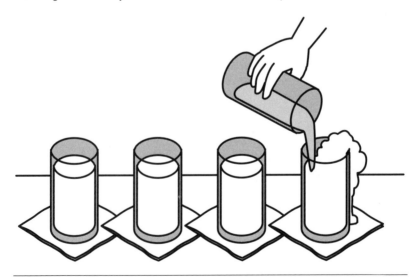

reaction. One glass at a time, add a couple of ounces of vinegar to each of the four glasses. Arrange your glasses so you pour the vinegar into the glass with the baking soda in it last. When the vinegar and baking soda come into contact with each other, you will see a chemical reaction which will consist of a lot of foaming. Be sure that you have something under all of the glasses. This will protect the surface you are working on. The glass with the baking soda in it will cause the most reaction. The others will have minimal reactions.

DISCUSSION IDEAS:

"What" Questions
- How similar did the four powders look?
- What happened when the liquid was added to each of the four powders?
- What criteria did you use to determine which powder you voted for before we added the vinegar?
- Was your criteria very useful?

"So What" Questions
- What can this activity tell us about knowing what is contained in a drug?
- Should we take the word of someone who gives us an illegal drug as to how safe it is? Why or why not?
- What is the drug dealer's reason for putting additional materials into a drug?
- What would some of the reasons be that people could react differently to the same drug?
- Do we really know how each person will react before they try a drug?
- Can we determine whether a drug is harmful for us? Why or why not?

- Whose decision is it whether you try a drug or not?
- What role do your peers play in deciding whether you will try a drug or not?
- What are some of the consequences of drug use?
- Who has to live with the consequences of the decision whether to try a drug or not?

"Now What" Questions

- How should we handle a situation where someone offers to let us try a drug?
- What reasons can you list for not trying drugs?

No Coupons

KEY WORDS: Responsibility, Cost, Earn

LOCATION: In your home

TIME ESTIMATE: 20 minutes plus discussion time

MATERIALS NEEDED:
- 10 - 12 grocery items from your house
- A piece of paper for each person
- A pen or pencil for each person

Concept

This activity isn't about how to make money, it's about the value of a dollar and the everyday cost of food. You've heard the old expression, "Money doesn't grow on trees." Well today it doesn't have to because kids think if you don't have enough money to buy something you just pull out the plastic and charge it. Therefore they aren't really concerned when you claim that you don't have enough money for something. Wasting food doesn't hit home to them since they don't equate food with money. This activity will give your kids a chance to experience the cost of food instead of just the experience of eating it. You want them to understand that cost isn't just the price you pay for an item, but it is really how long you had to work at your job to earn the money to pay for an item. Each person in our society has a responsibility to make an effort to provide for their needs.

Activity

Choose ten to twelve grocery items from your cupboard, refrigerator or freezer. Be sure that they reflect a wide variety such as meat, cereal, milk, cheese, dessert items, snack foods, etc. You will need to know the exact price (or at least a real close guess) of each item. You can either check the prices of the items you have at home the next time you go to the store, or you can keep track the next time you grocery shop and conduct this activity after you have completed your shopping.

Arrange the ten to twelve items on a table or counter. Give each participant a piece of paper and something to write with. Present each item to them one at a time. Have them guess how much the item costs and write their guess down on their piece of paper. Give each of your items a number or keep them in order so you will know which item they have priced on their piece of paper. Have them total up all of their guesses to get a total cost of all ten items. After you have presented them with all ten items, reveal the price of each item individually. See who has the closest guess on each item. Then at the end give them the total price of the ten items and see who was closest to the correct total.

DISCUSSION IDEAS:

"What" Questions
- How hard was it to guess the price of each item?
- Were your guesses usually high or low?
- Did you guess the exact price of an item? Which one?
- Which item were you the farthest from the correct price?
- What item was the hardest for you to guess? The easiest?
- How close did you come to the total cost?

"So What" Questions

- Why was it hard to guess the prices of these items?
- How could you get better at guessing the prices?
- What does this activity tell us about the cost of food?
- What does this activity tell us about wasting food?
- Is food more expensive to cook at home or buy ready to eat? At a restaurant?
- How do we get the money that is spent on food?
- How many hours would you have to work at minimum wage to buy all of this food?
- How can we control the amount of money we spend on food?

"Now What" Questions

- What does working and eating food have to do with each other?
- How should we treat the food that is in our kitchen?

Not Close Enough

KEY WORDS: Respect, Responsibility, Individuality, Role Model, Unique, Characteristic

LOCATION: In your living room or yard

TIME ESTIMATE: 15 minutes plus discussion time

MATERIALS NEEDED:
- A quarter for each person
- 1 magic marker
- Masking tape, string or something similar
- One measuring device such as a tape measure, yardstick or ruler
- 1 piece of paper and a pen or pencil for each person

Concept

Our youth culture places too much emphasis on looking cool. People who buy $100 sneakers just because they are named after someone famous, or try to lose weight to look like the superstars in a magazine, really need to look at their value system. Trying to be like someone else promotes a lack of self-esteem, unfair comparison, and a goal that is not only unrealistic, but impossible to reach. Each of us is unique, and we each have qualities that make us special.

Having role models is not a bad idea, as long as the person is someone that we can respect, not just someone famous. What qualities do they have that you wish you had? It is these qualities that we strive for, not to outwardly appear to be a carbon copy of that person. However, even as we strive for the positive qualities that these role models possess, we need to realize that we will be putting our own personal stamp on those qualities. We can respect another person, but we can not copy the other person. The unique characteristics that we already have can be enhanced by respecting others and trying to emulate others, but we can never be that other person. Our responsibility is to make ourselves the best that we can be.

Activity

If you have a room in your house that is large enough for this activity you can do it indoors, if not then take the activity outside. Give each person a quarter. Have each person use the magic marker and put their initials on both sides of the quarter. Use masking tape, string or something similar to designate a starting line, a line five feet from the starting line and a line ten feet from the starting line.

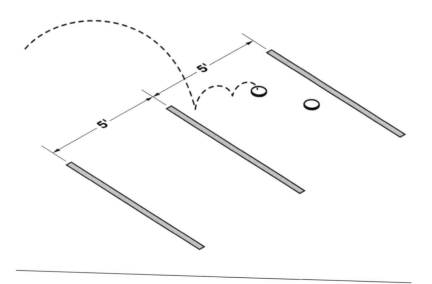

Explain that the activity begins with one person standing at the starting line and tosses their quarter so it hits somewhere between the five and ten foot lines. It may roll from where it hits, but it must stop rolling somewhere in between that distance. If it rolls past the lines, then the person must toss again. Then each person goes to the starting line and takes a turn tossing their quarter. They are trying to get their quarter to land as close to where the first person's original quarter stopped as possible. After everyone has tossed their quarter, use your measuring device and measure how many inches away from the first quarter each person's quarter landed. Round the distances to the nearest half an inch. Have each person record their distance. Everyone will record a distance from the original quarter except for the person who threw first.

Now repeat the activity with a different person being the one to toss the first quarter. Conduct enough rounds that each person gets to be the first thrower at least once. If you have time, you may let everyone be the first thrower more than once. Have each person add their own distances together for each throw that they make. For example, you might be 6 inches away in round one and 4 inches away in round two. This would give you a total of 10 inches for the two rounds. Keep individual totals through all of the rounds. The person who has the lowest score when you end is the winner.

DISCUSSION IDEAS:

"What" Questions
- How hard was it to get close to the original quarter?
- Was it easier when the quarter was closer or farther away?
- Did you get better the more times you tossed the quarter? Why or why not?
- Did you learn any tricks that made you score better?

- Would you rather be the first thrower or one of those trying to get close? Why?

"So What" Questions
- What are some areas in life where we try to be close to someone else in looks or abilities? Give examples.
- How easy is it to be like someone else?
- Why would we want to be like someone else?
- How close can we really come to being like someone else?
- What is the difference between looking or acting like someone else and being ourselves?
- What makes each of us unique?
- What is one positive characteristic of each person here in our group?
- Does being rich, famous, athletic, or beautiful make you a good role model? Why or why not?
- What is the difference between being famous and being respected?

"Now What" Questions
- Why is it difficult to model ourselves exactly like someone else?
- How can we develop our own individuality?
- What are the characteristics we should look for in a role model?
- What can we do to gain the respect of others?

Picasso

> **KEY WORDS:** Responsibility, Communication, Unclear, Vague, Feelings
>
> **LOCATION:** In your home
>
> **TIME ESTIMATE:** 10 minutes plus discussion time
>
> **MATERIALS NEEDED:**
> - A piece of paper for each person
> - A pen or pencil for each person
> - A self-drawn picture of a bug

Concept

Communication is an important factor within any family. When communication is vague or ambiguous, problems can occur and those problems can lead to anger. When a parent tells their child to clean their room, what does that really mean? Do they want the room spotless or do they just want all of the dirty clothes picked up and put in the wash? When a child tells their parents they will be home soon, does that mean ten minutes or an hour? Unclear communication can lead to behavior that doesn't meet the needs of either person. How many times have we thought someone should have understood what we wanted done and then gotten angry when the task wasn't completed exactly as we wanted? By being clear with what you say you can avoid a lot of problems and angry feelings. It is the responsibility of each person to be sure that what they say is clear, and it is the responsibility of the person who is listening to be sure that they understood not only what was said, but what was meant.

Activity

Before the activity starts, you will need to draw a picture of a bug on a sheet of paper. When you draw your bug, be sure that it has a head, body, two eyes, two antennas, two wings, four legs, a tail with a stinger attached, a second method to defend itself in addition to the stinger (such as claws on the feet) and decorations on its back. Don't worry if the drawing isn't a work of art - you will see later that it really doesn't matter. Do not let anyone see your bug picture.

Now bring the family together. Give each person a piece of paper and a pen or pencil. Explain that they are going to draw a bug. However, tell them that you have certain requirements for the bug and will be giving them instructions. Have everyone draw as you read the instructions. Tell them not to get behind or ahead of you. Pause briefly after each instruction to give them time to draw. Do not answer any questions about what you have asked them to draw. If they ask you a question about an instruction, tell them to do the best they can.

Here are the instructions:

1. Draw the body of the bug.
2. Draw the head of the bug.
3. Draw the legs of the bug.
4. Draw the wings of the bug.
5. Draw the eyes of the bug.
6. Draw the antennas on the bug.
7. Draw a tail with a stinger on the bug.
8. Draw a second method of defense for the bug (the first method was the stinger).
9. Decorate the back of the bug.

When the drawings are completed, have each person give their own drawing a letter grade (A to F) according to how good they think their bug looks. Now have them exchange pictures and give a letter grade according to how well they think the other person drew their bug. Exchange pictures one more time. However, instead of having them grade the picture on how well they think the person drew their bug, bring out the sample bug picture that you drew ahead of time and explain that this is a picture of the perfect bug. Have each person grade the picture they are now holding based on how well the bug <u>exactly duplicates</u> your perfect bug. For each item that is different, their grade goes down one grade. Return the pictures to their owners and have everyone compare pictures to see how well each of them did.

DISCUSSION IDEAS:

"What" Questions
- What was the letter grade you gave yourself?
- What was the letter grade you gave during the second round of grading?

- What was the letter grade you gave when comparing a drawing to the perfect bug?
- How well did you think you were following directions as they were given?
- Why didn't your bug turn out exactly as the perfect bug picture?
- What difference would it have made if the perfect bug picture had been shown to you as you were drawing your picture?

"So What" Questions

- What can this activity show us about communication?
- What happens when poor communication takes place?
- Has something like this ever happened to you or your friends? Explain.
- How do you feel when someone doesn't do what you told them to do?
- How do you feel when someone is upset with you when you didn't do what they asked?
- Whose fault is it when someone misunderstands you?
- Whose fault is it when you misunderstand someone?
- Who gets mad when there is a communication mix up?

"Now What" Questions

- What are some ways we can be sure people understand what we have said?
- How can we be sure we have heard someone correctly?
- Why is clear communication important in a family?

The idea for this activity was suggested to me by Lana Coombs. Thanks Lana!

Post Office

KEY WORDS: Perseverance, Responsibility, Goals, Worry, Past, Present, Future, Measurable, Prediction

LOCATION: In your home

TIME ESTIMATE: 15 minutes plus discussion time (one month later)

MATERIALS NEEDED:
- Paper and a pen or pencil for each person
- Mailing envelope and postage stamp for each person

Concept

We all have to deal with the past, present and the future. To be honest, there is not much we can do about the past. It is over and there is nothing we can do to change it. In the present there seems to be a lot of energy spent worrying about things that may happen. The future is full of promise. Alcoholics Anonymous use a prayer written by Reinhold Niebuhr that is called the Serenity Prayer that addresses worry. The prayer goes like this, "God grant me the serenity to accept the things I cannot change, the courage to change the things I can and the wisdom to know the difference."

We can do a lot to influence what takes place in the future. Successful people have indicated that part of their success came from having written goals that kept reminding them of what they thought was important. This activity combines the worries of today with the promise of the future. Goals can help us ignore the small petty problems that each day brings and concentrate on our future and what we want to become.

Activity

Give each person some paper and a pen or pencil. Even if you have a word processor or a typewriter, this activity is best done by hand. This gives you more time to think and has a more personal appeal. Explain that you want each person to write a letter to themselves. In the first part of the letter write down the date, the weather and what you did today.

In the second paragraph, write about things that are worrying you. It could be a class in school, an upcoming test, a problem you are having with a friend, or a situation with money or at work. Describe the problem in enough detail that you will be able to remember what it was one month from now. Talk about who is involved in the problem, what the situation is and some possible outcomes that could take place. Write down what the consequences could be for each of the possible outcomes. Predict which outcome you think will most likely take place.

In the third section of the letter have each person write down some goals they would like to accomplish during the next month. Be sure that the goals are written specifically enough that you can tell if they were in fact completed. For example, a poorly written goal would be, "I will read more. " This is vague and you would have trouble measuring it. A better way to express this goal would be to write, "I will read for 15 minutes a day during the next 30 days." Another poor example would be, "I will do better in school." A more measurable goal would be, "I will complete my homework before watching television." Don't let your family members write too many goals. Two or three good goals will be easier to work on than a list of five or ten wishes rather than measurable goals. Have them copy the goals onto another piece of paper. These goals should be posted in a place where they will see them often. Seeing them repeatedly will remind your kids of what they are trying to accomplish. Do not post the goals in a place where the whole world will see them. The refrigerator is not a good place. Possible locations would be their bedroom mirror, the bathroom or next to their bed.

Now have your kids address an envelope to themselves, put the letter inside, seal it and put a stamp on it Put the letters in a safe place. Write a reminder to yourself to drop these in the mail box in thirty days. Now it is true that you could just give them the envelopes back in thirty days, but there seems to be something special about actually receiving mail. When your kids receive the letter, they can review the things that were worrying them one month earlier. They can see if they were worrying needlessly about something that never even took place or how accurate they were with their predictions as to how things would work out. They can review their goals that they set for the last thirty days and see how successful they were at reaching their goals.

The discussion for this activity will not take place until after the letters have been received in the mail. This is an activity that can be repeated as many times as you like. The letters give each person a shorthand diary about their life. Your family may save the letters for future reference. You can lengthen the time frame to more than thirty days on subsequent letters. Keep the intervals relatively short for the first few letters so they will get used to the process.

DISCUSSION IDEAS: (One month later.)

"What" Questions
- Did you enjoy getting mail? Why or why not?
- How hard was it to think up things that were worrying you?
- How hard was it to think of the different outcomes that might happen?

- How hard was it to think up the goals that you wanted to accomplish?
- How hard was it to write your goals so you could measure them at the end of thirty days?
- How often did you read your list of goals during the month?

"So What" Questions

- How accurate were you with your predictions about what would happen to the things you were worrying about?
- Did any of the things that you were worrying about fail to take place?
- How often do we worry about something that never takes place?
- Describe a situation that you or a friend had where something you worried about never took place?
- Have you ever had a situation that you worried about where when it actually happened it was not as bad as you predicted? Describe such a situation.
- How well did you do in reaching your goals?
- How difficult was it to reach your goals?
- What are some of the barriers that got in your way when you were working on your goals?
- Did having your goals written down help you to work on them?
- Do you always have to be successful in reaching your goals to consider the attempt a success?
- What happens when you don't have goals?

"Now What" Questions

- Why doesn't worrying help us solve our problems?
- Which problems in our life should we concentrate on finding solutions for?
- How can sitting and writing down goals help us reach our dreams?

Reach For The Stars

KEY WORDS: Perseverance, Responsibility, Goal Setting, Achievement

LOCATION: In your home

TIME ESTIMATE: 10 minutes plus discussion time

MATERIALS NEEDED:
- Masking tape
- A wall
- A tape measure or yardstick
- A pen or pencil

Concept

In every area of our children's lives we want them to be the best that they can be. This could include their schoolwork, athletics, church programs and any other areas in which they are involved. This activity can be used to discuss the fact that no matter how well they are doing right now, they could probably do better with a little more effort. Maybe the problem isn't that they need to try harder, but they need to try "smarter." If they are studying in front of the television set for one hour and they want to improve their grades, maybe spending two hours studying in front of the television set wouldn't be as beneficial as spending only one hour studying without the television. Sometimes it's not the amount of effort we put into a project as much as it is how smart we are about that effort. Rather than just trying harder to reach your goals, think about what you can do differently to reach your goals.

Activity

Ask each participant to stand next to a wall and reach up the wall just as high as they can. While doing this they must keep their feet flat on the floor. Explain that this is not a competition against each other since there are obvious height differences between your kids. Place a piece of masking tape on the wall to mark the highest point they were able to reach. Measure how high the mark is from the floor and write that distance on the masking tape on the wall. Have each person do this one at a time so the other participants can watch them. Participants should be spaced along the wall so no one is reaching over or under someone else's piece of masking tape.

After everyone has had a turn, have each participant try again and see if they can reach any higher than they did the first time. Have them stand right under their first mark so they will be able to see how well they did the first time. Remember that they must keep both feet flat on the floor. Once again mark the highest point they were able to reach. Measure how high the mark is from the floor and write that distance on the masking tape. Most people will be able to beat their first attempt.

Now explain that on this third attempt, instead of standing flat, they may hop or jump on one leg to see if they can reach higher. If you have a high enough wall you can let them use two legs to hop or jump. Mark these attempts with masking tape. Measure how high the mark is from the floor and write that distance on the masking tape. Once again, they should be able to reach higher with their hop or jump than they were able to when they had to stand with their feet flat on the floor and just reach.

DISCUSSION IDEAS:

"What" Questions
- How high did you reach the first time?
- How high did you reach the second time?
- How high did you reach when you were able to jump?

"So What" Questions
- Why were you able to reach higher the second time?
- Would you agree that you tried harder the second time? Why or why not?
- Did having the masking tape there give you something to shoot for?
- Why were you able to reach even higher when you were allowed to jump?
- What can this activity tell us about "trying harder"?
- How can having specific goals help us to achieve more?
- How was the jumping attempt different than the reaching attempts?
- Explain this statement: "If we always do what we've always done, we'll always get what we've always got."

"Now What" Questions
- What can we do instead of just "trying harder" to reach our goals?
- How can thinking or acting differently help us to achieve our goals?

Restaurant Voice

KEY WORDS: Caring, Respect, Manners, Etiquette, Polite, Appropriate

LOCATION: In your home at dinnertime

TIME ESTIMATE: 30 minutes plus discussion time

MATERIALS NEEDED:
- Fancy dinner setting
- Candlelight
- The dinner meal

Concept

One time when I was eating dinner at a nice restaurant, I was seated next to a family with a number of children. At one point during the evening the kids were becoming somewhat loud. The mother at the table said, "Remember kids, you need to use your restaurant voices." This got me to thinking about appropriate behavior and that leads to manners. We all want our children to behave appropriately when they are out in public, but have we given them the proper guidelines so they know what we expect? We need to take time at home to let them know what we mean by appropriate behavior.

You will have to decide what you expect from your children and let them know what that is. For example, decide if you want them to use the words "please" and "thank you," not interrupt someone else when they are talking, wait until everyone is served before starting to eat, keep their elbows off of the table, use their napkin, not talk with their mouth full, take only the amount of food they can eat, speak quietly, etc. I have seen many lists of what we are supposed to do, but the lists aren't as important as you deciding what you would like for them to do. Once you have let the kids know what your expectations are, you need to provide opportunities for them to practice. Even though this activity is going to use dinnertime as the place to practice manners, make your children understand that the same behavior is expected outside of dinnertime. I believe that manners are really a form of respect. Their proper use reflects an awareness of how we feel about other people. It shows that we care enough about them and their feelings to behave in an appropriate manner.

Activity

This activity starts with you deciding which mealtime manners you would like to emphasize. Make a written list and give it to everyone in the family. Number each one of the rules. Review the list with them before dinner and explain what you expect. Don't make the list too long. If you need to you can add to the list and repeat the activity again at another time while focusing on the additional behaviors. Tell them that you will be having a special dinner and they are to practice these behaviors during the meal.

Prepare a special dinner and set the table as fancy as you can. Candlelight is a nice touch. Have everyone dress up for dinner. Have them bring their copies of the list with them to dinner or post a large copy somewhere in the room where everyone can see it. As you serve dinner, allow each person to make a comment when someone, including the adults, forgets one of the rules. This reminder should not be done in a harsh or critical manner. A comment such as, "Nicole, rule #4" will do.

Follow up activity: After you have had your special dinner, follow it up by inviting a guest over to have dinner with your family. Remind everyone of the rules before dinner, but do not comment during dinner when someone breaks one of the rules. You may comment after the guest has left.

DISCUSSION IDEAS:

"What" Questions
- Were any of the rules new to you? If so, which ones?
- How hard was it to remember the rules during the dinner?
- How much effort did you make to watch and see if someone else broke a rule?
- How did the fancy table setting and atmosphere make you feel?
- Did good manners make the meal take longer?

"So What" Questions
- How did these rules affect dinnertime?
- Is being polite hard to do?
- How do other people react to people who are not polite? Who are polite?
- Should you only use good manners at certain times? At home? At school?
- What are some good manners that we didn't talk about that you think are important?

"Now What" Questions
- Why is it important to practice good manners?
- Which of these rules would be useful at times other than mealtime?
- How does the use of good manners show respect for others?

Ring Toss

KEY WORDS: Perseverance, Goal, Achieve

LOCATION: In your home

TIME ESTIMATE: 20 minutes plus discussion time

MATERIALS NEEDED:
- A pen or pencil
- 2 blindfolds
- 3 canning jar rings
- Masking tape

Concept

Setting goals helps people achieve their dreams. Research has shown that people who write their goals down will achieve a higher percentage of their goals than individuals who think about goals but neglect to write them down. Writing goals down helps to clarify your thinking. Once we have set our goals, it is time to begin working on them. Too many people try to reach their goals without using all of the resources available to them. Working hard isn't always the answer; working smart is sometimes the answer. Part of working smart when you are trying to reach a goal is to search out people who can help you. These individuals may be experts at what you are trying to do or they may be willing individuals who would just like to help. No matter what your goals are, you can usually reach them faster and easier if you seek help from others. However, for others to help you, they must know what you are trying to achieve. If you don't ask for help and share your needs, then others can't be of much assistance.

Activity

Use the masking tape and make two lines on the floor one foot in length. The lines should be about six feet apart and parallel to each other. This activity takes five rounds. Divide into teams of two. If you have uneven numbers, one person can be on two different teams.

Have each team keep a total combined score of how many rings they get over the pencil in all five rounds. Each ringer is worth five points. The thrower and the catcher must always remain behind the masking tape lines. Their hands and arms may go over the line, but not any other part of their body. In each of the five rounds have both team members take a turn at being the thrower and the catcher.

In round one, both the thrower and the catcher are blindfolded. The catcher will take the pencil and hold it on the floor on one of the lines of masking tape. The thrower will stand on the other line of masking tape and make three tosses with the rings and attempt to get the rings over the pencil. After the ring has been tossed in the air, the catcher may move the pencil to attempt to capture the ring. Since neither one of them can see, this will prove to be difficult. Before moving on to round two, be sure both people on the team have had a chance to be both the thrower and the catcher.

In round two, have only the catcher be blindfolded. Once again the catcher may move the pencil to try to help get the ring over the pencil.

In round three, no one is blindfolded. But the catcher may not move the pencil. It must remain stationary on the masking tape as the thrower tries to get the rings over the pencil.

In round four, again no one is blindfolded. The catcher must start with the pencil on the masking tape, but as soon as the ring is in the air the pencil may be moved to help capture the ring. The pencil must return back to the masking tape before the next throw is made.

The fifth round is the same as the fourth. However, between round four and five, stop the action and have a discussion as to what strategies can be used to improve the scores. The team with the highest score after all five rounds is the winner.

DISCUSSION IDEAS:

"What" Questions
- How well did you do in each round?
- Did your scores get better as the rounds progressed?
- What made rounds one and two so difficult?

- Was round three any easier since you could both see, but the catcher couldn't move the pencil?
- How did you do when the catcher could move the pencil?
- How easy was it when you were the catcher and could help by moving the pencil?
- Did the catcher improve in round five over round four? Why or why not?
- What strategies did you discuss between rounds four and five?
- Did the strategies help improve your score in round five?

"So What" Questions

- The goal was to get the ring over the pencil. Did this become easier when someone else was helping you?
- Do you think it is important to have goals in your life?
- What happens when you don't have goals?
- Is it OK to change your goals even after they have been set? Why or why not?
- When you set a goal, do you think you could reach it easier if someone else helped you?
- If you never share your goals with anyone, will they be of much help to you?
- How can people help you in reaching your goals?
- What kind of person would you want to help you reach your goals?
- How would you go about choosing a person to help you reach your goals?
- Would you choose different people for different goals? Why or why not?

"Now What" Questions

- You knew what your goal was in this activity. Do you know what your goals are in life?
- What goals do you have for this week? This month? This year? The next five years?

- Who can you ask to help you reach your goals?
- How can you be the one to help others reach their goals?

Follow-up

Have everyone write one goal that they would like to reach in the next week and one for the next month. After each goal have them write down the name of a person who can help them reach that goal. Then post these written goals in a conspicuous place where they will see them everyday. This could be the start of a long lasting practice that will help them throughout their lives. This process is much more effective if the adults in the house do it also.

Shake Rattle and Roll

KEY WORDS: Perseverance, Work, Effort, Task, Goals, Success, Reward

LOCATION: In your home

TIME ESTIMATE: 20 minutes plus discussion time

MATERIALS NEEDED
- A small container of heavy whipping cream
- A small glass jar with a lid
- Salt
- Crackers or rolls
- A table knife

Concept

Work and play are both four letter words, but there is a world of difference between the two for most people. The word work means putting out effort. At first some jobs or tasks may seem fun but as time goes on those same tasks become routine, dull and boring. At that point we can all agree that what we are doing moves from play to work. This could be anything from sports to homework. How we react to work will determine our level of success in life.

Most rewards in life do not come without a long period of effort. A college degree comes only after seventeen years or more of effort. A sports star is born only after years of dedicated practice. A business succeeds only after long hours and sleepless nights. Successful inventions come only after any number of failures. Perseverance is the key to many of our successes. If we give up just because things get tough, then we may never accomplish our goals. "When the going gets tough, the tough get going" is really true. If your children develop the value of working through the tough times and continuing to strive to reach their goals even if doing so means hard work, then nothing can stop them

Activity

In this activity your family is going to make butter. Before beginning the activity you will need to buy some cream. In the dairy section of your grocery store you will find small containers of heavy whipping cream. Do not buy the ordinary whipping cream; be sure it is designated as "heavy". You will need a small glass jar with a lid. You can use a baby food jar or something larger. Begin by pouring the heavy whipping cream into the glass jar. Fill the jar about half full. You need to leave room for the cream to move as you shake the jar and to allow the cream to expand as it turns to butter.

Now begin to shake the jar vigorously. Have everyone take turns shaking the jar. Allow each person to shake until their hand becomes tired. If they are shaking with just one hand, do not let them switch hands; let this be the signal that it is the next person's turn to shake the jar. After two or three minutes, stop and open the jar up to see what changes have taken place. Then put the lid back on and resume shaking. Continue to open the jar up every two or three minutes to see what is happening. When almost all of the liquid cream has turned to a solid, you are done. Pour the slight amount of excess liquid out of the jar. Sprinkle a little salt in the jar. Put the lid back on and shake it a few more times to spread the salt evenly. Again pour off any excess liquid. Now get out some crackers, rolls or popcorn and enjoy the fruits of your labor.

DISCUSSION IDEAS:

"What" Questions
- How hard was it to shake the jar?
- How did your hand or arm feel after you shook for a while?
- How did the cream look the first time you opened the jar? The second time? The third time?
- How long did it take to turn the cream into butter?
- How did the butter taste?

"So What" Questions
- What would have happened if you completely stopped shaking as soon as the first person's arm was tired?
- What would have happened if you stopped shaking after two or three minutes and never started again?
- How did spreading the work among more than one person help you make butter?
- What can making butter teach us about reaching our goals?

- Should we quit just because a task becomes hard? Why or why not?
- How can others help us when a task or assignment gets tough or hard to do?

"Now What" Questions
- Whose responsibility is it to be sure that we complete a task?
- How does effort and hard work help us reach our goals?
- What are the rewards of completing a task?

Sherlock Holmes

KEY WORDS: Caring, Respect, Stereotyping, Judging

LOCATION: In your home

TIME ESTIMATE: 20 minutes plus discussion time

MATERIALS NEEDED:
- A piece of paper for each person
- A pen or pencil for each person
- A variety of objects that you have collected
- A description of three different people
- 3 grocery bags

Concept

How do we form our opinions of others? Many times we let first impressions influence what we think. These first impressions may be based on a person's clothes, the way they talk, where they live, their religion or the color of their skin. However, how accurate are first impressions? Have we based our impression on things we have believed about how a group of people look and act? Do we put people into categories such as "preppies," "jocks," "nerds," "stoners," etc. based only on what we see?

One way to respect others is to care enough about them to take the time to get to know them before making judgments about who they are and what they think. When you lump everyone into stereotypical groups based on what you see, you reduce them to a one-dimensional definition instead of the complex person that they really are. We should not draw conclusions about a person based only on what we see or hear about them.

Activity

Prior to starting the activity you will need to do some planning. Look around your house and gather up a number of items that could belong to a fictional person that you are going to create. Let me give you an example of the kinds of items I would collect. The items would be things that I would find in a person's bedroom. They could include: a fishing bobber, a hunting knife, a leather keychain with the name Tom stamped into it, a compass, an address book with a religious symbol on the front and a pair of men's glasses.

After collecting the items, I would create a fictional person to go along with these items. The items would reflect the following about this person: the person is a female, she is a teenager, she likes to fish, hunt and hike, she has a lot of friends, she is religious, she has a boyfriend named Tom and her father left his glasses in her room last night. Since the items don't always reflect something specifically about the person, you can create anything that fits the items you have collected. Notice that I tricked the group by using the pair of men's glasses. These did not belong to the person, but were found in her bedroom. As you gather the items and create the fictional characters, you want them to be vague enough that there will be many interpretations of what the person is like based on the items you show. As you will see, it won't be until the third round when they can ask questions that their lists will be close to the created person's characteristics.

Repeat this process of collecting items and creating a person twice more. You should end up with items and descriptions for three characters. Put the items for each person into a separate bag so no one can see them until you are ready.

It is now time to gather the family together. Give each person a piece of paper and a pen or pencil to write with. Explain that you are going to show them a number of items that you found in a fictional person's bedroom. Their job is to take on the role of a detective and try to figure out as many things about the person as they can based on the items that you are going to show them. Tell them to be as specific in their characteristics as possible. You would like for them to try and decide if the person is a male or female, their age, what their likes or dislikes are, what they do with their free time, any physical characteristics that they can determine, etc.

Begin by bringing one item at a time out of the bag. Let them take a look at the item, but do not answer any questions about the item. After bringing it out of the bag, place the item on the table or the floor where everyone can see it. Once you have brought everything out of the bag, give each person about two minutes to write down as many characteristics as they can determine about the person as possible. When the two minutes are over, have them read their lists out loud. Now you read your list of characteristics and have them give themselves one point for each characteristic they wrote down that matches a characteristic you made up. The person with the most correct matches is the winner of that round. Repeat the activity a second time with new items and a new fictional description.

Repeat the activity a third time with new items and a new fictional description. However, after showing them the items but before having them make their list of characteristics, allow them to ask you ten questions about the person that can be answered "Yes" or "No." Anything they find out during the question and answer time can be used to make up their list of characteristics.

Discussion Ideas:

"What" Questions

- How much trouble did you have thinking of characteristics?
- Was your list longer or shorter than the lists of others? Why?
- How precise were you when you listed your characteristics?
- How well did you match the correct characteristics on the first two rounds?
- How hard was it to think of questions about the person to ask?
- How much easier was it to list characteristics after you were able to ask questions?

"So What" Questions

- Why was it easier to list characteristics after first asking questions?
- How much do you know about a person when you first meet them?
- What do you judge a person on when you first meet them?
- What kinds of mistakes can we make when we judge a person by just what we see?
- What is wrong with generalizing about a person by how they look or who they hang out with?
- Is hearing about a person from someone else a good way to get to know them? Why or why not?
- How does getting to know someone show that you care about them?

"Now What" Questions

- What is the best way to get to know someone?
- What is wrong with drawing conclusions about a person using just a few bits of information?

Stop Watch

KEY WORDS: Caring, Respect, Responsibility, Consideration, Apology, Reliability

LOCATION: In your home

TIME ESTIMATE: 10 minutes plus discussion time

MATERIALS NEEDED:
- A watch with a second hand on it
- A piece of paper
- A pen or pencil

Concept

Time plays a major role in how our society functions. One of the ways we show respect for others is to respect their time. When we have agreed to meet someone at a certain time and we do not show up at the appointed time, we are basically saying that what they have to do is not as important as what we were doing. It is our responsibility to be aware of our schedule and to keep an eye on the clock. By being considerate of others' time, we show that we care about them and their needs. If something is going to delay us, then a phone call is always appreciated. If something unavoidable does occur, then an apology is appropriate. Not being considerate of the time of others shows an uncaring attitude on our part. Planning ahead and being reliable goes a long way in convincing others that you are a responsible individual who respects others.

Being on time for an appointment or for a job is not the only way time is important to us. Meeting a deadline is also part of being responsible. When you miss a deadline it impacts others who are counting on you to complete your part of the job before they can finish what they have to do.

Activity

This activity is done individually. Explain that the activity involves estimating time. You will give the participants a time to shoot for and they will try to guess when that much time has passed. You begin the round by giving them a time (such as sixty-five seconds) that they are trying to estimate. When you say "begin," start keeping track of the time that has expired. While the clock is ticking, you or any other player may distract the participants by asking them a question, singing or some other distraction. The purpose of the distraction is to make it harder for them to count off the seconds in their head. They should raise their hands when they think the right amount of time has gone by. Do not tell if they are right or wrong until everyone has finished making their estimate. As soon as someone raises their hand, indicate on your piece of paper the time that has actually passed. Do not let anyone see what the actual time was until everyone has made their guess.

Once everyone is finished guessing, tell each person how much time had actually passed when they told you to stop. The person that was closest to the correct time is the winner of that round. Repeat this process for four or five rounds, changing the time they are trying to guess for each round. The person with the most correct guesses is the winner. You may also have a grand prize winner that was closest to the correct time after combining all the rounds. To do this, you must keep track of how many seconds away from the actual time each person was in each round and add their rounds together to get a total score. The smallest score wins.

DISCUSSION IDEAS:

"What" Questions
- How close were you to the correct time?
- Were your guesses usually low or high?
- How many rounds did you win?
- Did you get better the more rounds we played?
- Was it easier to guess shorter or longer times? Why?
- What method did you use to try to keep track of the passing time?
- Did you change your strategy as we went along?
- Did your new strategy work better for you?
- Did the distractions bother you?

"So What" Questions
- Why is time important in our society?
- What happens when someone ignores time?
- What problems can be caused when one person is late for an appointment?
- How does it show a lack of respect when you don't arrive on time?
- How important is it to complete assignments on time?
- What happens when we miss a deadline?
- How does our being late impact others?
- How does our missing a deadline hurt others?
- If you turn your school work in late, what could the consequence be?
- If you have a job and always arrive late, what could the consequence be?
- How does being on time make you more responsible?

"Now What" Questions

- What methods can you use to help you arrive on time?
- What steps can you take to help you complete a job on time?
- How can being aware of time help you gain the respect of others?

Storyteller

KEY WORDS: Cooperation, Creativity, Problem Solving, Compromise

LOCATION: In your home

TIME ESTIMATE: 15 minutes plus discussion time

MATERIALS NEEDED:
- 20 small pieces of paper with a couple of extras (about 2 inches by 3 inches)
- A pen or pencil for each person
- A paper bag (You could also use a hat or a box)

Concept

Individual effort is appreciated, but working with others is critical in today's world. We work in teams, groups and committees all of our lives. Very few of us will work or live in a situation where we have the final say on everything. How well we are able to take the ideas of others and blend them with our own ideas will determine the success we have when working with other people. One skill that helps when being asked to work with others is creativity. Many times the solution to opposing opinions or ideas is a creative combination of those opinions. Compromise is made up of taking two different approaches to an issue or problem and looking at many different answers before deciding on one that will work in that particular situation.

Activity

Give each person a pen or pencil. Take ten small pieces of paper and divide them equally among the participants. If the papers can not be handed out equally, give the extra papers to the older kids. Ask each person to write one word on each of the pieces of paper that they were given. They are to write a different word on each piece of paper. Ask them to write clearly so others will be able to read their word. Tell them to not show the word that they wrote on their paper to anyone else. Place a paper bag in the middle of your group and when each person finishes writing their words, they should put them in the bag. When completed, you will have ten pieces of paper with ten different words. Without showing anyone the words, take them out of the bag and read through them silently. If by chance there are duplicates, you can use one of the extra pieces of paper to substitute a different word. Then place the ten pieces of paper back into the bag.

Explain that this is going to be a storytelling activity. To begin, have one person select a piece of paper from the bag. After they have selected, have the person on their left select a piece of paper from the bag. The first person that chose a piece of paper will start telling a make believe story out loud. As they tell their story, they must at some point use the word they have drawn in the story. They may continue to tell the story after they have used their word or they may stop at the end of the sentence that has their word in it. However, each person must continue the story for at least thirty seconds. When they are finished, the person on their left picks up the story where they left off and continues it. As with the first person, they must at some point use the word that they drew from the bag in the story. When they begin, have the next person draw a word from the bag so they will be ready to go as soon as the story gets to them. Continue in this fashion until all of the words are drawn. Remind the last person that they must draw the story to some kind of conclusion.

Repeat the activity starting over with a new set of words.

Discussion Ideas:

"What" Questions

- How hard was it to think up words to write on the piece of paper?
- How hard was it to use the word you drew in the story?
- Did the story make sense?
- How did you feel when your turn was next?
- If right before your turn the story started to go a direction you hadn't planned on, what did you do when it was your turn?

"So What" Questions

- How hard was it to pick up where someone else stopped in the story?
- Was the activity easier the second time around? Why or why not?
- Would it have been easier if you could have done the whole story by yourself?
- What part does cooperation play in this activity?
- Is it always easy to cooperate? Explain.
- Why is cooperation important?
- What part does compromise play in cooperation?
- Does someone have to be the winner and someone the loser when we compromise? Why?
- How can creativity help us solve problems?
- Does creativity help us cooperate with one another?

"Now What" Questions

- What kinds of behaviors do we show when we are cooperating? When we are not cooperating?
- When there are two opinions about how to solve a problem, how can we use cooperation, creativity and compromise to come to an agreement?

Thank You

KEY WORDS: Caring, Thank You, Special, Encouragement, Support, Role Model

LOCATION: In your home

TIME ESTIMATE: 20 minutes plus discussion time

MATERIALS NEEDED:
- Two pieces of paper per person
- A pen or pencil per person
- An envelope per person
- A postage stamp per person

Concept

"Thank you" is easy to say, but sometimes hard to put into written words. I would, of course, suggest that you require your kids to write thank you notes to those who send presents or money. Written thank you notes are becoming things of the past and I find that disheartening. Phone calls and e-mail have replaced the hand written thank you that means so much to many people. There is still a certain thrill and spirit of excitement when you receive something in the mail that isn't a bill or hasn't been sent by some company trying to get you to send them your money.

However, this activity goes beyond a simple thank you. This calls for thanking someone who has made a difference in your life. We all have certain people who go out of their way to make our life a little more special. They have shown us that they care, not by just what they say, but by their actions.

Activity

Each of us have people in our lives who make us feel special. This could be a coach, a teacher, a Boy or Girl Scout Leader, a Sunday School Teacher or other religious leader, a relative, a good friend, etc. You know who I'm talking about. Think of a special person either now or in your past that has made a difference in your life. Someone who took a special interest in you and ended up making such an impact that your life was different because of that person. I'm getting a warm feeling even as I write this thinking back over all of the people who fit this category in my own life. Even though people such as these don't do what they do expecting to be rewarded, this activity honors those people and their efforts.

Describe to your family a few of the people who helped you in this way. Explain what a difference they made in your life and what you would have missed had these people not taken the time and made the effort to help you along. The help could have taken the form of encouraging you to fulfill your potential, of patiently teaching you a skill, of supporting you through a hard time, of being there when you needed them, of being a role model, of making you feel significant and important, or of simply caring about you as a person. After you have finished talking about people who helped you, ask each person to make a list of the people who have helped them in the past and are helping them now. After each person's name, have your kids write down what these individuals have done to get on their list. After the lists are complete, share them with the family.

Now have each person pick one individual from their list and write them a thank you letter. The letter must be handwritten.

Typewriters, word processors and computers have their place, but this letter should come from the heart, and nothing says that like handwriting. The letters should be very specific. Instead of just saying "thank you for all you have done for me," the letter should describe what they have done, how it made you feel and what difference it has made in your life. It doesn't have to be long, but it does have to be personalized, specific and from the heart. Then mail the letter to each special person.

This is an activity you can repeat from time to time. The activity gives each of us a chance to realize that we do have people outside of our immediate family who care for us and are concerned with our well being. I have been on both ends of this activity. I have written thank you letters and received them. They have a great impact on both the writer and the recipient.

DISCUSSION IDEAS:

"What" Questions
- How hard was it to think of people who have meant a lot to you?
- What kinds of things had they done to get on your list?
- How long was your list of special people?
- Did you have trouble deciding which person to write the thank you letter to?
- How hard was it to write the letter?

"So What" Questions
- Why would we want to write these people a letter?
- How do you think the person will feel who receives your letter?
- How did you feel while writing your letter?
- How would you feel if someone wrote this type of letter to you?
- Do you think these people help others so they will receive thank you letters? Why or why not?

- What makes these people special?
- How are these people role models?

"Now What" Questions
- Why is it important to say "thank you" to people who support and encourage us?
- How can we help others like these people have helped us?

The Big Picture

> **KEY WORDS:** Responsibility, Decision, The Bigger Picture
>
> **LOCATION:** In your home
>
> **TIME ESTIMATE:** 15 minutes plus discussion time
>
> **MATERIALS NEEDED:**
> - 1 blank piece of paper for each person
> - Crayons or colored pencils
> - A large picture from a magazine
> - A pair of scissors

Concept

Kids want to experience as much as they can. They want to stay out late, visit with friends, go lots of places, etc. You as the parent have to be the one who says "No" when what they want to do is unsafe. To your kids a party is just a fun get-together of friends. To the parent a party is trouble waiting to happen. We have to worry about drinking, drugs, sex, violence and a whole list of other problems that could occur. So while your child is thinking about the fun when they ask to go, you are thinking about the trouble when they ask to go. This obviously sets up a conflict between you and your child.

You are looking at the big picture while they are looking only at the fun. This same scenario plays itself out in a number of other areas. You want them to do well in school so they can go to college or get a good job and be happy. They are more worried about what their friends are thinking. We need to get them to expand their thinking from the "here and now" to the bigger picture. They need to understand that a number of factors play a part in making a decision, and these factors must be taken into consideration if you are going to make a good decision. Decisions that are made from a narrow focus or with very little information don't allow you to make an informed decision.

Activity

Find a picture in a magazine that has very little or no writing on it. The picture should have a lot of things going on in it. It should also be large enough that you can cut it into a number of pieces without the pieces ending up being too small. Do not let anyone in your family see what the entire picture looks like. Cut the picture out of the magazine. Cut the picture into the same number of pieces that you have people in your family. Place the pieces of the picture face down on a flat surface.

Have each person in the family choose one of the pieces. Tell them not to let anyone else see their piece of the picture. Give each person a blank piece of paper. Have them glue their piece of the picture onto the center of the paper. Have them go to separate areas of the room and add to the picture by drawing. They will need to determine what they think the rest of the picture might have looked like. Their challenge is to make their picture look as much like the original as possible. If they received a piece that had a barn, they might draw farm animals and a farm house. If they received a piece that had a front porch, they would draw the rest of the house and surrounding area. Let them be creative and add whatever they think the rest of the picture would look like. Give them about 10 minutes to add to their picture. After you call time, have everyone gather and share their pictures. Then gather the original pieces together to determine what the original picture looked like.

DISCUSSION IDEAS:

"What" Questions
- What did you add to your picture?
- What were the clues in your piece of the picture?
- How close were your additions to the real thing?
- Could you have added more to the picture if given more time?

"So What" Questions
- How hard is it to determine everything from just one little section of the picture?
- How easy would it have been if you had seen the entire picture before starting to draw?
- When making decisions, how much information would you like to have?
- Are we always able to know everything before making a decision?
- How can we get more information?
- What is meant by the term "the bigger picture"?

"Now What" Questions
- What should we do when faced with making a decision with only a few facts?
- How can we keep ourselves from making decisions without considering the bigger picture?
- Who could we turn to for help in making a decision?
- Who could we turn to for help in seeing the bigger picture?

There's Only One You

> **KEY WORDS:** Respect, Self-esteem, Unique, Characteristics, Diversity, Similar
>
> **LOCATION:** In your home
>
> **TIME ESTIMATE:** 10 minutes plus discussion time
>
> **MATERIALS NEEDED:**
> - #2 (or softer) pencil for each person
> - 3 inches of transparent tape for each person
> - 2 pieces of blank white paper about 3 inches by 3 inches for each person

Concept

Respecting yourself is important. We are all unique and have different qualities that make us special. It is this being different that allows our society to function as well as it does. Without differences, we would not have the combination of abilities and varying insights to invent and create the things that we need. We need to celebrate these differences and unique characteristics.

Respect for ourselves also means that we don't have to be like everyone else. Pressure from our peers to be like them shouldn't be what influences our behavior. Respect for ourselves says that we will eat healthy, exercise, stay away from harmful drugs and not put ourselves in situations that may become violent.

Activity

Begin by having each person use a pencil and color a space a little larger than their thumbprint on a white piece of paper. They should use a lot of lead when coloring. Use a soft-leaded pencil. Have them turn the pencil so the side of the lead can also be used. Be sure that the area is heavily coated with lead. Now have them take their thumb and press it down firmly on the lead covered area. They should roll the thumb firmly so that the entire thumb area where the thumbprint is located is thoroughly covered with pencil lead.

Now have each person take a piece of tape and put it on the thumb over the thumbprint area. Be sure that the tape is put on smoothly for best results. Once the tape has been placed on the thumb, take it off the thumb and stick it on a clean white sheet of paper. On the paper you will be able to see the thumbprint through the tape. Anywhere the tape was not placed smoothly on the thumb, a clear area will be left on the tape.

Have family members compare their fingerprints with each other. Now repeat this activity using other fingers in addition to the thumb.

DISCUSSION IDEAS:

"What" Questions
- What do you notice about your thumbprint?
- Do you notice anything that stands out and is easily recognizable on your thumbprint? Explain.
- How does your thumbprint compare with those of others?
- How does your thumbprint compare with other fingers on your same hand?

"So What" Questions

- How can we compare fingerprints to the characteristics of people?
- Fingerprints are hard to see. What are some characteristics that are easy to see?
- List ways in which people are the same. Are different.
- How do these characteristics help to make everyone different?
- How can people be similar but not the same?
- Why is it important to have different types of people in your town or city? In your school?
- Why is it important to have different types of people as your friends?
- If we were all the same, what kind of a world would we have? Explain.
- How does being different help us sometimes and hurt us sometimes?
- Do people always respect how unique each of us are? Explain.

"Now What" Questions

- How should we treat others who might be different than we are?
- List some behaviors that show respect for ourselves.

Uppers and Downers

KEY WORDS: Caring, Respect, Feelings, Tone of Voice, Body Language

LOCATION: In your home

TIME ESTIMATE: 15 minutes and then 2 or 3 days plus discussion time

MATERIALS NEEDED:
- Piece of paper that you can hang up and use as a scoreboard
- A written list of fruits and vegetables

Concept

Respect for others involves not only what we think of people, but how we treat them. One of the major factors in how we treat others is the words that we say. The words we use have the ability to make people feel good or "up," and they can make people feel bad or "down." The tone of voice and the body language we use when we tell someone something also lets people know if the words we are using are "up" words or "down" words. I have noticed with our dog that I can say, "Come here wonderful dog" in a nice sweet voice and he will come right over. I can say the same thing in a mean voice and he hangs his head and slinks away. It isn't always the words we use as the way we use them.

Activity

Before the activity, write up a list of about seven fruits and vegetables. For example, you could use tomato, pineapple, banana, orange, lima beans, eggplant and apple. After the family gathers, explain that we will be playing a game similar to charades, except that talking is allowed. You will ask someone to read this list of fruits and vegetables in such a way that their tone of voice and their body language will allow us to guess what emotion they are trying to get across. Choose your first person and whisper the word "funny" to them. They will now read the list of fruits and vegetables in such a way that the rest of the group can guess that the emotion they are trying for is "funny." Tell the group that they will try to guess the emotion while the person is reading the list. Continue with others using emotions such as mad, in love, happy, bored, sleepy, etc.

Once you have completed the first part of the activity, explain that words and the way we say them have an impact on us. Some words and phrases make us feel good; we will call these "uppers." Some words and phrases make us feel bad; we will call these "downers." For the next few minutes have the group brainstorm words and phrases that make them feel "up" and some that make them feel "down." Examples of "up" words and phrases would be "Thanks, you really helped me," "Way to go," "You're really smart," "Your hair looks good today," etc. Examples of "down" words and phrases would be "Stupid," "You Jerk," "You can't do anything right," "Get out of my way you idiot," "Shut up," etc.

After coming up with a list of "up" and "down" words and phrases, let them know that for the next two or three days everyone will be keeping track of how many times they use "up" and "down" words and phrases. The word or phrase must have the proper tone of voice and body language for it to be an "upper." Someone can't say, "You are an idiot" in a nice tone of voice and consider it an "upper"; it would still be a "downer." Make a score-board on a piece of paper. List everyone's name and make two columns. The first column will be labeled "up" and the second column will be labeled "down." Put a pen or pencil by the score-board for easy access. During the time period you have chosen, anyone who hears someone using an "up" or "down" word or phrase will go to the scoreboard and put a mark under the proper category by the name of the person who said the word or phrase. If two or more people hear the word or phrase, only one person marks it down. Even though you are only keeping track of what takes place at your house, ask the kids to be aware of how their friends and other adults talk to each other.

At the end of your two or three days, total up the marks and see who in your family helps others by trying to make them feel good and who needs to work on respecting others more. Take anyone out for ice cream who has used more "uppers" than "downers."

Discussion Ideas:

"What" Questions
- Did you end up with more marks for "uppers" than "downers"?
- How hard was it to remember to use words that made people feel good?
- How hard was it to avoid using words that made people feel bad?
- Did you go out of your way to say good things? Why or why not?
- When listening to your friends and adults, what kind of words and phrases did you hear?
- How often did you hear each other say "downer" words out of habit?
- How often did you hear each other say "downer" words just to join in with the rest of the crowd?

"So What" Questions

- How do "upper" words and phrases make you feel when you hear them about yourself? "Downer" words and phrases?
- How do other people react when you use "upper" words and phrases? "Downer" words and phrases?
- How do the words we use show that we respect other people? That we don't respect them?
- How can words show that we care for others? That we don't care?

"Now What" Questions

- What can this activity teach us about the words and phrases that we use?
- What does language have to do with respect? With caring?
- How can we show others that we respect and care for them?

Walking Dictionary

KEY WORDS: Responsibility, Knowledge, Definition, Vocabulary

LOCATION: In your home

TIME ESTIMATE: 30 minutes plus discussion time

MATERIALS NEEDED:
- A dictionary
- A piece of paper and pen or pencil for each pair of participants

Concept

There is a radio advertisement that says that "people judge you by the words you use." There are thousands of words in the English language, yet most of us rely on a small portion of them to get us through our daily lives. Words convey information, feelings, thoughts and opinions. They allow us to express ourselves easily and clearly. The reason there are so many words is because each one of them has a specific meaning and a particular use. Without a knowledge of a wide variety of words, we will be limited in our selection of which words to use. Part of many college entrance exams is a section where you match words with their definitions. The appropriate and articulate use of words identifies a person as one who is well educated and sophisticated. Each of us has a responsibility to improve ourselves. Education is one way of doing that. It is not just the school's job to educate us, it is our own responsibility to take advantage of any learning opportunity we can.

Activity

You will need to spend some time before the activity getting this one ready. Look up five words in the dictionary that your children will not know the definition of. Choose words that have a fun or unusual definition. Some examples would be:

Ulna: The larger of the two bones of the forearm on humans on the side opposite the thumb

Circada: Large flylike insects with transparent wings

Mazzard: A wild sweet cherry

Tetragram: A word having four letters

Vibrissa: Stiff hairs growing near the nose of animals such as cat's whiskers

After writing down the word and the correct definition of the word, make up two other incorrect definitions for each word. Some examples would be:

Ulna: A large load carried by an animal.
A tool used to repair the ukulele, a musical instrument.

Circada: To go around the world.
To divide something in half.

Mazzard: A cousin of the buzzard.
A traffic accident involving more than one car.

Tetragram: A telegram sent by satellite.
A five sided drawing.

Vibrissa: What a string does on a musical instrument.
A seasoning put on Italian food.

Find enough additional words with fun or unusual definitions so you will have one for each participant. Write each of these words and its correct definition down on its own separate piece of paper. You will end up with a piece of paper for each person. Do not make up phony definitions for this second set of words.

After finding your first set of words and creating two phony definitions for each, you are ready to begin the activity. Give each participant a piece of paper and a pen or pencil. Read each word and the three definitions, the correct one and the ones you have made up. Do not always read the correct definition first or last; change the order in which you read them. Have each person write down on their piece of paper which definition they think is the correct one. They can just write down if it was the first, second or third one you read; they don't need to write out the definition. After you have gone through all five words, go back over the words and the definitions. After reading the choices for each word, give them the correct answer. For each correct answer guessed, they receive 100 points.

Now pass out the second set of words and the correct definitions which you wrote down on separate pieces of paper. Give one to each person. Have them create one or two phony definitions for their word. When everyone has finished creating their definitions, have each person take a turn reading their word and definitions. Once again have the other participants write down their choice for the correct definition. When everyone has read their word and definitions, go back and reveal the correct answers. For each correct answer guessed they receive 100 points. In this round, the person making up the phony word definition receives 100 points for each incorrect guess that was made about their word.

When the activity is completed, explain that it's not really over. You are going to give the family one new word on each of the next seven days. If your children span a wide range of ages, give them different words. Everyday give each of your children a piece of paper with the new word and definition written on it. Post the word and its definition in obvious places around your house such as the refrigerator, television set and bathroom mirror. Their challenge is to learn the correct definition of that word and try to use it properly as many times as possible during that day. Each night discuss how they were able to use the word. Nightly you should also review the previous definitions that you have already done. Don't use unusual words like you did during the activity. Choose words that will improve and expand their daily vocabulary. If you need some word suggestions, the Reader's Digest has a monthly section called "Word Power" where you could get some ideas. You could also choose some from current newspaper or magazine articles that tie into current events.

DISCUSSION IDEAS:

"What" Questions
- How high was your score?
- How many of these words have you heard before?
- How hard was it to decide which was the correct definition?
- What made you decide on one definition over another?
- How hard was it to make up your own definitions?
- What made it hard or easy for others to guess the word that you had?

"So What" Questions
- Why do we have so many different words?
- Why would we want to know the meaning of a large number of words?
- List some words that mean almost the same thing. (Mad-Angry, Happy-Pleased, Frustrated-Discouraged)
- Why is the proper use of words important?
- How can knowing a lot of words help us in our daily lives?
- What should we do if someone uses a word that we don't know the meaning of?
- How is it our responsibility to become educated?

- Who is more important at school, the student or the teacher? Explain your answer.

"Now What" Questions
- How can we expand our vocabulary?
- Why do we go to school?

What's That Sound?

KEY WORDS: Cooperation, Respect, Communication, Listen, Understand

LOCATION: In your house

TIME ESTIMATE: 20 minutes plus discussion time

MATERIALS NEEDED:
- Tape recorder
- Audio tape with sounds that you have prerecorded
- Paper and a pen or pencil for each person

Concept

Do we really listen to each other? True listening begins with actually hearing what another person has to say. This kind of listening is more than just hearing the words that are spoken. This kind of listening requires the person to not only listen, but concentrate on what is being said rather than just waiting for their turn to talk. Understanding comes from not just hearing the words, but hearing what the person is really trying to tell you. This means that we can't watch television, listen to our favorite radio station or read the newspaper and carry on a conversation at the same time. We need to concentrate on what is being said. When we listen with the purpose of understanding, we show respect for the other person and what they are saying. Cooperation begins with communication. Until you know what someone else wants you to help them with, it is hard to cooperate. Sometimes when someone thinks you aren't being cooperative the real problem lies with poor communication.

Activity

Before the activity, you will need to tape record various sounds. You will need to record nine to fifteen different sounds. The easiest way to do this is to make a list of sounds that you want to record and record them in that order. This eliminates the need to transfer the sounds to another tape to put them in the order that you want to play them.

Each sound needs to be recorded twice, with a period of silence between each recording. This period of silence will give you a chance to stop the tape recorder during the playback. These can be simple sounds such as a car horn honking, or they can be more difficult, such as a garbage disposal. Don't make them too easy. Have some that are really hard to guess. The activity will be played in three rounds. The sounds for each round should get progressively harder to identify. Some of the sounds I have used are a typewriter, car horn, alarm clock, popcorn popping, washing machine agitating, toilet flushing, someone eating a corn chip, sewing machine, telephone ringing, and a pencil sharpener. You are only limited by your own imagination.

Start the activity by giving each person a pen or pencil and a piece of paper. Explain that you will be playing a tape recording of certain sounds. Each sound will be repeated twice. Play the sound the first time and then give them time to think about what they heard. Now play the sound a second time and have them write down their answer. Repeat this process for all of the sounds that you have recorded.

Break the activity into three rounds. Explain that round one (the easiest of the sounds) is worth 100 points for each correct answer, that round two (the second third of the sounds) is worth 200 points for each correct answer and that round three (the most difficult of the sounds) is worth 300 points for each correct answer. Stop after you have completed each round. Give the correct answers after each round and let the participants see how they are doing.

DISCUSSION IDEAS:

"What" Questions
- How easy was it to identify the sounds that you heard?
- Did you usually identify the sound the first time it was played or the second time?
- What helped you to identify each sound?
- Which sounds were the easiest for you to identify?
- Which sounds were the hardest for you to identify?
- Did you listen harder to the 100 point sounds or the 300 point sounds? Why or why not?

"So What" Questions
- How can this activity be compared to communication?
- What does listening have to do with communication?
- How hard do we listen to others?
- How often do you listen as hard to another person as you listened to the sounds that were worth 300 points?
- List some of the people you really listen to?
- Why is it important to listen to others?
- How can poor listening lead to arguments and fights?
- What does communication have to do with cooperation?
- What kinds of things get in the way of listening to what others have to say?
- What types of body language do we use when we are really listening hard to someone?
- When someone really listens to you, how does that make you feel?
- How does it make you feel when you aren't listened to?

"Now What" Questions

- What can we do to make ourselves better listeners?

Other Activity Books
By Tom Jackson

Book covers and sample activities may be viewed at
www.activelearning.org

Don't miss out! Be sure you have all of Tom's powerful, hands-on activities and discussion techniques which you can use immediately to make a real difference in the lives of kids. Each book has different activities in them.

These activities and discussion strategies will create excitement and increased learning anywhere there is a group of kids. Thousands of professionals have successfully used these activities with elementary and secondary groups and have found them effective with inner city, suburban, rural, high-risk and at-risk populations. These fun, hands-on activities have been tested in the real world of classrooms, after school programs, churches, prevention programs, treatment centers, juvenile detention centers, etc.

Students learn best by doing! All of Tom's activity books contain user-friendly activities that get kids involved in their own learning process and let them have fun at the same time. The books include opening chapters on how-to use activities and tips for leading effective discussions. Each activity is followed by a list of questions that can be used to help you transfer what you did during the activity to real life applications. These activities can be used in classrooms, counseling and support groups, youth programs, after school programs, churches or anywhere else you would find a group of kids. Great for all grade levels!

Activities That Teach: 60 hands-on activities that address topics such as alcohol, tobacco and drug prevention, and which teach skills related to communication, values, working together, problem solving, stress management, goal setting, self-esteem, decision making and more. 234 pages. Retail price: $15.95 (Quantity discounts available)

More Activities That Teach: All different activities than Tom's first book. 82 additional hands-on activities that address topics such as alcohol, tobacco and drug prevention, and which teach skills related to anger management, resisting peer pressure, diversity, violence and gang prevention, communication, values, working together, problem solving, stress management, goal setting, self-esteem, decision making and more. 341 pages. Retail price: $18.95 (Case discounts available)

Still More Activities That Teach: 55 all new activities which address all of the topics from previous books, along with these new topics, conflict resolution, respect, responsibility, school-to-careers, team building, media influence and healthy lifestyles. Discussion questions at the end of each activity are divided into easy-to-use categories. 257 pages. Retail price $15.95 (Case discounts available)

Conducting Successful Group Discussions With Kids: A leader's guide to making an activity meaningful and educational! Discover a simple, yet effective four step discussion outline that is effective and engaging. Additional strategies include getting kids to talk, questions to ask, discussion formats to use, room arrangement, teacher tips, student behaviors and much more. Pages and retail price not available at time of printing. (Case discounts available)

For ordering information about any of Tom's books:

Call toll free (888) 588-7078
between the hours of 7:00 a.m. and 7:00 p.m. Mountain Time

Write: Active Learning Center
3835 West 800 North, Cedar City UT 84720

FAX: 435-586-0185
web site: www.activelearning.org
e-mail: staff@activelearning.org
Mastercard, Visa, Checks, or Purchase Orders gladly accepted

Educators, Counselors, Youth Workers and Others: *Hear Tom Jackson Live!*

That's right! Wouldn't it be great to have Tom come to your school or conference and share with you his creative, yet practical hands-on activities? Tom's activities have been described by teachers and others who work with children and youth as "Simply the best life skill activities I have ever used! They teach life skills in such a way that kids not only learn, but love doing them." Or you can broaden the topic by having Tom talk about active learning as a teaching tool which can energize any classroom or program.

Reading about the activities is exciting, but there is no substitute for actually doing them. Tom uses his "learn by doing" approach to walk you through a number of activities from his two books ***Activities That Teach*** and ***More Activities That Teach***. Here is a chance to ask questions, get insider tips and learn first hand how to process and discuss the activities with your kids. Hundreds of teachers, counselors, youth workers and others have participated in Tom's workshops, and one of the most common remarks is, "I wish we had more time. This is the most useful workshop I have ever attended."

Tom is available for keynote presentations, conference breakouts, workshops, teacher in-services, peer helper trainings, youth leadership programs and conferences. Funding sources that have been used successfully by other organizations include staff development, Safe and Drug Free Schools, Title I, At-Risk and High Risk, as well as special grants and community resources. Join up with a neighboring school, school district or organization and save money by sharing travel costs when Tom stays more than one day in your part of the country. We will even try to book another workshop in your area to help you save money on travel if you will give us other likely people to contact!

Give Janet Jackson a call at (435) 586-7058 and ask for Tom's speaker packet. This will give you more information concerning cost, travel and references. Or, just give Janet a call and suggest to her a person in your school district or organization who would be interested in hearing more about Tom and she'll contact them directly.

Parents, Parenting Instructors, Parent/School Organizations and Others Who Are Interested In Helping Families:
Invite Tom Jackson To Your Area

Help families help themselves! Invite Tom Jackson to make a presentation to the parents in your area. Tom doesn't conduct the usual parenting workshop where someone tells parents how they should parent. Instead, he gives parents easy to do, hands-on activities that can be done right in their own homes to open up the lines of communication and discuss important topics with their children in a non-threatening way. Tom also conducts workshops specifically for parenting instructors which focuses on how to facilitate parent trainings using Tom's activities.

Explore the values of Caring, Cooperation, Honesty, Perseverance, Respect, Responsibility, and Service to Others along with other topics too numerous to mention. Rather than telling you what to believe, the activities provide a user-friendly vehicle to allow each parent the opportunity to share their own values with their children No one said learning has to be boring! Spend time sharing your values with your children and having fun at the same time.

Reading about the activities is exciting, but there is no substitute for actually doing them. Tom uses his "learn by doing" approach to let you participate in a number of activities from his book *Activities That Teach Family Values.* Here is a chance to ask questions, get insider tips and learn first hand how to use the activities to discuss values with your kids.

Tom is available for keynote presentations, conference breakouts, workshops and evening presentations. These can be done for parents, trainers of parents or others who work with families. Another option is to conduct a workshop for parents and their children ages 7 to 15. Have them actually experience the activities together and see how much fun they really are!

Give Janet Jackson a call at (435) 586-7058 and ask for Tom's speaker packet. This will give you more information concerning cost, travel and references. Or, just give Janet a call and suggest to her a person in your school district or organization who would be interested in hearing more about Tom and she'll contact them directly.